TOUCH FOR LOVE

Also by Wataru Ohashi with Mary Hoover
published by Ballantine Books

NATURAL CHILDBIRTH, THE EASTERN WAY

TOUCH FOR LOVE

Shiatsu for Your Baby

by Wataru Ohashi
with Mary Hoover

Ballantine Books · New York

To our son,
Kazuhiro John Ohashi

Library of Congress Catalog Card Number: 85-90585

ISBN: 0-345-30090-4

Cover design by Georgia Morrissey
Cover photo by Suzanne Szasz
Text design by Holly Johnson
Manufactured in the United States of America

First Edition: February 1986

10 9 8 7 6 5 4 3 2 1

Contents

1 · Why Massage Your Baby?

As a father, I know what it is like to cope with having a new baby in your home. I understand the tremendous emotional and physical demands this puts on both parents. Considering how hard it is for new parents to find time for doing all that needs to be done, why massage your baby?

For the Fun of It

The obvious reason for doing this is the pleasure it gives both of you. Once you experience this, you may need no further reasons for massaging your child regularly. Still, it's nice to know that what is such fun is also good for your baby in other important ways. Five more benefits to your child are described here.

Emotional Well-Being

The most prevalent kind of sensory stimulation throughout prenatal life is tactile. The amniotic fluid and sac encasing the fetus provide an unborn baby with what amounts to an almost continuous soothing massage. Viewed in this context, the importance of being lovingly touched to a baby's emotional well-being is easy to appreciate. Not only does such touching soothe and emotionally reassure infants and young children, it may well be crucial to survival in the early months. Studies of infants in institutions have shown that unless their caretakers devote some time every day to cuddling them lovingly, the babies fail to thrive, even though their purely physical needs are adequately met.

Better Health

The method of infant massage demonstrated in this book is based on principles of traditional Oriental medicine utilized in *shiatsu*— sometimes called acupressure or "acupuncture without needles." Giving a shiatsu massage to babies involves gentle stroking instead of the pressure used with adults, but the theoretical underpinnings are the same. These will be explained in the next chapter. All that needs to be said here is that a shiatsu massage not only tones skin and muscles, but also stimulates internal organs, helping to promote and maintain their healthy functioning. Thus, it offers a unique way to regulate involuntary activities, such as circulation and digestion. It has been used in the East for thousands of years to foster all-around good health and prevent serious illness.

Sound Physical Development

During infancy and early childhood, regular shiatsu massage also helps ensure good development of all a child's organs and bony structures. At this time of life, when growth proceeds at such a rapid pace, minor skeletal distortions and organic difficulties can easily develop—and be easily outgrown, under favorable circumstances. Shiatsu both encourages sound physical development and helps a child outgrow any slight developmental problems that may occur. It also alerts parents to such conditions early (see chapter 7).

Cognitive Growth

Regular massage even promotes cognitive growth. A Texas hospital that prescribes massage for premature infants found that a group who were massaged regularly during their hospital stay and for four months afterward tested significantly better in neurological development and mental functioning than a control group who were not massaged. This finding that pleasurable tactile stimulation is good for a baby's brain bears out the traditional Eastern view that your child's development is all of a piece. Physical, emotional, and mental development are intricately interrelated. What affects one aspect of growth, or one part of the body, ultimately affects all. Hence the Oriental belief in "holistic health and healing"—the view that no problem or part of the body can be successfully treated in isolation, that to bring about lasting improvement anywhere, the person as a whole must undergo changes that result in better or more harmonious functioning all around.

Parent-Child Closeness

Not surprisingly, the hospital study mentioned in the preceding section also found that in the group of premature infants who received massage, the mother-child relationship was significantly enhanced—considered a good sign for a child's future development and happiness. In this instance, only mothers were taught to massage their babies. I recommend that fathers do it also. It is a great way to help care for your baby and strengthen the bond between you.

Parents Benefit, Too

Obviously, the rewards are not all on one side. An enhanced, parent-child relationship is a plus for parents as well as for the child. There are many ways you can benefit from massaging your baby. Knowing that you contribute simultaneously to your baby's pleasure and health is very rewarding. So is watching how your child responds—whether with wide-eyed concentration, smiles, coos, delighted wriggling, or a dreamy look of utter contentment. In addition, giving a massage has a calming effect on the person doing it, just as on the person receiving it. As your hands glide over your baby's skin, everyday problems and frustrations temporarily recede. You just concentrate on your child. At the end of a ten-minute massage the two of you should be serene and happy together.

In the days after my son was born, as I gave him shiatsu I increasingly felt he was the one of us who was giving most—giving me affection, teaching me how I was born and how I was raised and how I am attached to my ancestors and connected to future generations. I recognized that much as babies need their parents, parents also need their babies. Through the daily activities that provide your baby with protection, care, and love, you confirm your linkage to the universal human tree. For this reason, in Japan a baby is sometimes thought of as a "hinge." Taking care of your baby helps you to know where you came from and where you are going.

The Eastern View of Health

I would like to change parents' attitudes toward sickness and the other physical disorders so common during early childhood. In Western thinking, getting sick has a negative connotation. It implies a kind of failure. This attitude grows out of the Western tendency to think in terms of opposites: If you are sick, you are not healthy. If you are not sick, you are healthy.

Eastern thinking is different. Getting sick is considered part of the process of becoming or staying healthy. From this viewpoint, children can get sick but still be healthy. And a person who is never sick is not necessarily healthy.

In the east, shiatsu has traditionally been used as a way to foresee and ward off health problems before they become really serious. Chapter 7 of this book offers some shiatsu procedures for keeping track of your child's physical status from day to day. In chapter 9 you will find some traditional shiatsu remedies for common problems of infants and young children. These are natural remedies that stimulate the body's own recuperative powers.

The name *shiatsu* comes from two Japanese words: *shi,* meaning finger, and *atsu,* meaning pressure. Though this name is relatively new, approximately a century old, the art itself has been practiced in the Orient for thousands of years. It is a method for stimulating specific points located all over the body to foster health and healing and relieve tension and pain. Appropriate stimulation is provided through pressure, stretching, and various other means. Since the method is based on the same theoretical concepts as acupuncture, it is often referred to as "acupuncture without needles."

The Holistic Approach to Health

Shiatsu, like all Oriental healing arts, grows out of a holistic theory of health. According to this thinking, the functioning of all our body's organs and structures is intimately intertwined. The well-being of each body part ultimately both affects and depends upon what is going on everywhere else. Hence, no health problem is ever treated in isolation. It is believed that, to bring about lasting relief from any difficulty, the total picture must be taken into account, including life-style and emotional state. Many different organs and functions may need stimulating to create a healthier equilibrium throughout the body.

Of course, Western medicine does not differ absolutely on this score. In the West today, many problems are viewed as due to a combination of emotional and physical factors. Attention is increasingly focused on the role of diet and exercise in treating and preventing a variety of ills. Still, holistic thinking puts much more stress on the pervasive interaction of everything about a person's functioning.

This difference accounts for the fact that shiatsu therapy often involves stimulating areas of the body far removed from what, to Western eyes, is the site of a particular difficulty. For example, one of the procedures recommended in this book for improving your child's appetite and digestion calls for rubbing down the front of both legs from hip to ankle. This procedure will become understandable as you read the text and look at the illustrations.

Meridians, Tsubos, *and* Ki-energy

Some of the technical material in this section may initially strike you as formidable or alien. Don't be intimidated by it. Actually, you don't have to know anything about the Eastern concepts explained here in order to follow my program of infant massage. The procedures to use with your child are all quite simple and are explained in the following chapters in plain language with clear, step-by-step illustrations.

However, I include the technical material so that you will understand the thinking behind these procedures—know why you do what you do. You don't have to master this background material unless you want to. It is there for you to refer to whenever you wish. Just read through it before going on to the rest of the book, then use it for reference purposes as you see fit. You may be surprised to find how quickly you absorb the gist of it without even trying.

From ancient times Orientals have defined the functioning of the human body in terms of *yin* (passive) and *yang* (active) dynamics. The body is animated by a vital life force, or *ki*-energy, which is channeled through fourteen interconnecting pathways, or meridian lines. These meridians govern the functioning of the body and link the organs. There are seven yin and seven yang meridians, forming seven complementary pairs.

In terms of the information that follows, it is essential to remember that the yang meridians run downward toward the toes, while the yin meridians run upward toward the head and the fingers.

In giving a shiatsu massage, you "go with the flow," that is, you move down yang meridians, up yin ones. To get this right when working on a person's arms, you must always imagine them to be extended straight up overhead, as shown on pages 6 and 7.

The fourteen meridian lines are named and illustrated on pages 7 through 14. All the meridians except "governing vessel" and "conception vessel" exist on both the left and right sides of the body, though for the sake of clarity, the illustrations show them on one side only.

The names of some meridians do not correspond to Western definitions of organs or body functions. "Triple heater" describes the mechanism for producing heat and delivering it to various parts of the body. "Heart constrictor" is involved with circulatory functioning. "Governing vessel" and "conception vessel" oversee and balance the energy flow in the other twelve meridians. It should also be pointed out that "spleen" does not mean the organ of that name, but the general function of the spleen and pancreas.

Along each meridian line there are many "pressure points," or *tsubos,* which, when adults are being massaged, may be stimulated individually through sustained and often deep pressure. However, with babies and young children, just tracing the meridian lines provides all the stimulation to the tsubos that is needed. Only rarely in this book do I suggest stimulating a specific tsubo, and then just with light circular massage, or a "jiggling" motion. So the following illustrations show the location of only a few of the body's numerous tsubos. They appear as dots on the meridian lines with numbers next to them, and their position is further explained in the captions accompanying the meridians.

According to Eastern thinking, proper stimulation of the tsubos promotes a balanced flow of ki-energy throughout the body to maintain healthy overall functioning. If the flow of this vital force is somehow impeded anywhere in the body, illness or other problems occur. Healing requires restoring the flow, through massage and other techniques.

Meridian Lines and a Few Tsubos

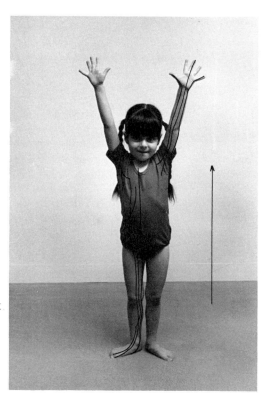

Yin Meridians, Seen from Front

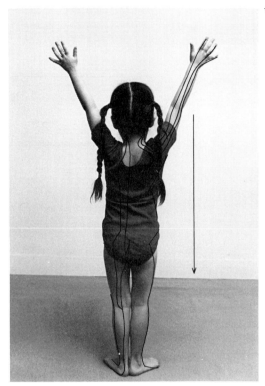

Yang Meridians, Seen from Back

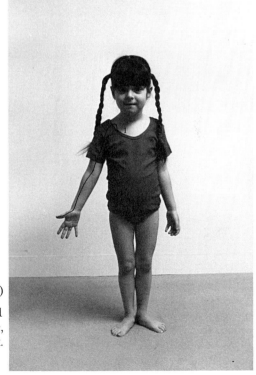

Lung Meridian (Yin)

Lung #1
Location: Just below the collarbone,
slightly above and to inside of armpit.

Large Intestine Meridian (Yang)

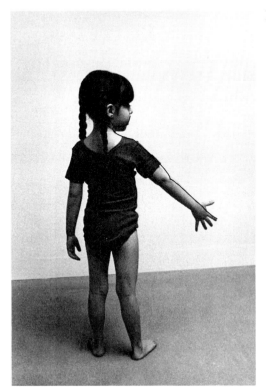

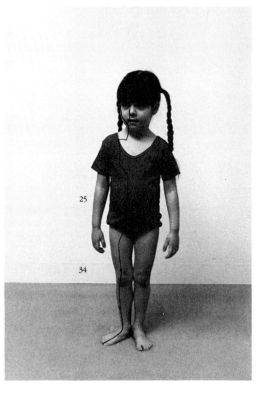

Stomach Meridian (Yang)

Stomach #25
Location: Level with the navel and
about an inch to each side of it.

Stomach #34
Location: A little above the top of the
kneecap and slightly to the outside of
the center of the leg.

Spleen Meridian (Yin)

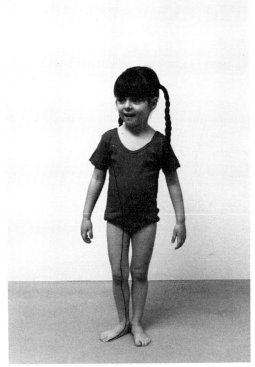

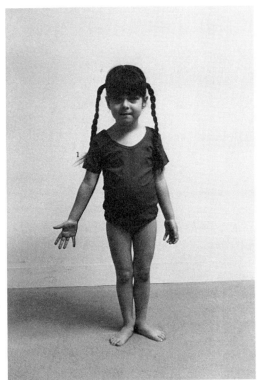

Heart Meridian (Yin)

Heart #1
Location: Just above the armpit.

Small Intestine Meridian (Yang)

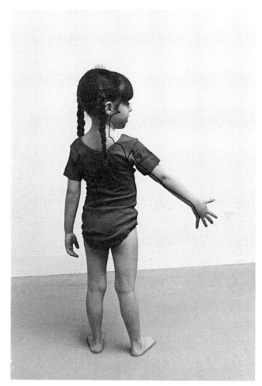

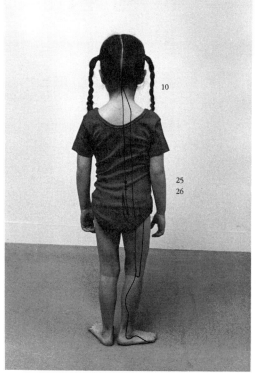

Bladder Meridian (Yang)

Bladder #10
Location: At the back of the neck, just
below the head and on either side of
the spinal column.

Bladder #25
Location: On either side of the spine
and slightly above the level of the top
of the pelvic bone.

Bladder #26
Location: On either side of the spine,
level with the top of the pelvic bone.

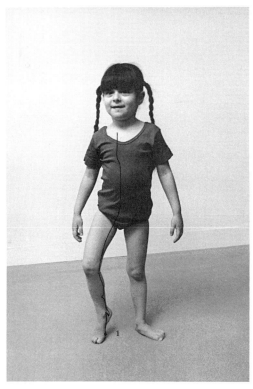

Kidney Meridian (Yin)

Kidney #1
Location: On the sole of the foot,
midway across it and just off the ball of
the foot, toward the arch.

Heart Constrictor Meridian (Yin)

Heart Constrictor #8
Location: In the center of the palm.

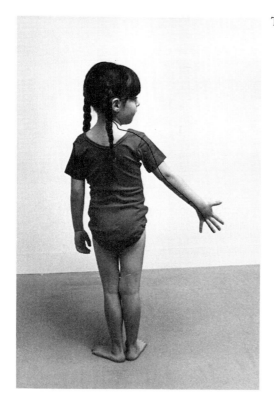

Triple Heater Meridian (Yang)

Gall Bladder Meridian (Yang)

Liver Meridian (Yin)

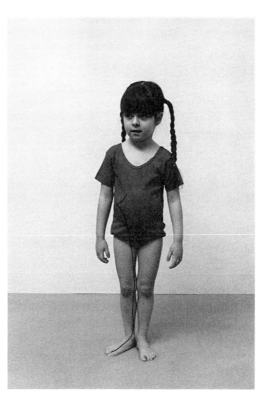

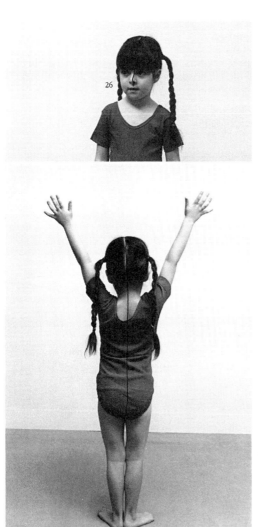

Governing Vessel Meridian, Front and Back (Yang)

Governing Vessel #26
Location: Just below the bottom of the nose.

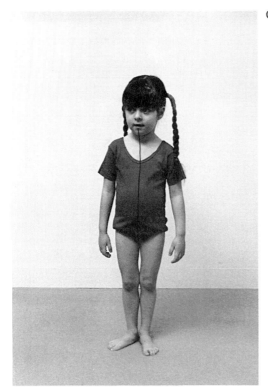

Conception Vessel Meridian (Yin)

3 · Guidelines for Giving Shiatsu to Babies

It is safe to begin some of the routines demonstrated in this book as soon as your newborn's navel is healed. Others should not be used until after the age of four months, or whenever your baby becomes adept at lifting and holding his head and shoulders up steadily when in the prone position. A breakdown of what procedures to use at various ages follows. If you have any question about your child's readiness for any of the more advanced routines, consult your physician.

For Infants Under Four Months

- Give gentle all-over massage as described in chapter 4.
- To vary your massage from time to time, add any of the four routines in chapter 5.
- Use any of the diagnostic procedures in chapter 7.
- Use any shiatsu remedy for common problems in chapter 9 *unless it is preceded by an asterisk (*)*

For Babies Over Four Months

- Continue to give a complete massage, but enrich it by introducing any of the alternative massage techniques in chapter 6, switching off among them.
- Use any routines in chapter 5.
- Use any diagnostic procedure in chapter 7.
- To spice up your program, include any of the exercises in chapter 8, switching off among them.
- Use any of the shiatsu remedies for common problems in chapter 9.

For Toddlers

- I recommend continuing a regular massage program until your child is about three years old. Ideally it should include a complete daily massage, plus a few exercises (chapter 8) that appeal to you and your toddler; some will have been outgrown. You need not devote more time each day to your program than you did earlier, just substitute more energetic routines for some of the gentle stroking suitable for newborns.
- Use any routines in chapter 5 that you and your child enjoy.
- Use any diagnostic procedures in chapter 7.
- Use any shiatsu remedies for common problems in chapter 9.

The Proper Setting

A basic, complete massage needs to be given on a rigid surface, such as a changing table or pad on the floor. The latter is safer, as soon as your baby begins to roll over and "travel." It also affords a larger working area, which is desirable with older babies. Your own bed, unless you sleep on a firm futon on the floor, usually is not rigid enough to be suitable. Though some procedures can be done while you are seated in a chair or on a sofa with your child on your lap, or even when you are standing and holding him in your arms, these positions are not appropriate for giving a full massage.

Soft background music may help to set the stage for a massage and keep you and your child in the right mood throughout. However, keep the volume low enough so that you can sing or talk to your baby when you feel like it.

Your child should be naked, at least if you plan to give a full massage, and for most other procedures in this book, too. Direct contact with a young child's skin provides more effective stimulation. Also, being nude simulates life in the womb more closely and therefore makes any massage or exercise a more emotionally rewarding experience for your young one.

This means that the room where you massage your child should be warm and free of drafts. Even in hot weather, avoid directly exposing your unclothed offspring to a strong breeze, from a fan or through an open window or door.

Though young children usually love being naked in a suitably warm and draft-free setting, a few infants object loudly during the first few weeks of their lives. Infants' tolerance for the change in temperature varies greatly from individual to individual. Special sensitivity to being naked is physiological and will be outgrown in time. Meanwhile, parents of such a baby should not subject their child to this unpleasant experience. Often such sensitive infants will let you undress them without protest provided a diaper or light receiving blanket is kept tossed over their midriff. If this works with your baby, he can be massaged—and sponge bathed—this way. But don't undress him completely for a massage if this distresses him.

Since a baby is likely to make a good massage the occasion for a good pee, it makes sense to place some waterproof material between him and the surface on which he is being massaged, but not touching his skin, please. Cover the waterproof fabric with a cotton sheet. Also, you may want to keep a diaper handy to deal with accidents.

Follow Your Child's Lead

Having a massage should be a pleasant experience for your child. So pick a time when your baby is happy to massage him, and stop if he becomes cranky. This rule applies—except in a few instances noted below—to using all the procedures in this book.

The exceptions are the routines suggested in chapter 9 for calming a cranky or crying child and relieving the discomfort of teething and colds. Parents tend instinctively to use massage to soothe an upset or sick child. I offer some traditional shiatsu procedures for this. However, don't continue with a procedure if your baby does not begin to respond positively within a minute or so.

Preparing Yourself to Massage Your Child

Giving a massage should be an enjoyable activity for you, not a chore. Try to choose a time when you feel serene and unhurried. If your response to that last sentence is "Ha!" believe me, I do recognize how busy parents of young children are. Nevertheless, busy as we may be, there are times when we just put aside everything and play with our babies. These are good times for a massage. Interestingly, just deciding to massage your baby often has the effect of putting you in the proper mood. Or music played softly may do the trick.

Be sure that your nails are well trimmed and smoothed with an emery board. (A wise precaution any time you will be handling a naked baby.)

Warm your hands before touching your unclothed child. (Again, not only when giving a massage.) You can do this by putting them in warm water for several minutes or by rubbing the palms together briskly. Cold hands give a naked baby a most disagreeable shock.

You can position yourself in numerous ways to massage your baby, as shown in the following chapters. The only requirement is that you get into a position in which you will feel comfortable and relaxed for up to ten minutes and which will enable you to reach the entire length of your child's body easily. If you are going to sit on the floor and are not accustomed to doing so, I suggest that you support your back with a pillow against a wall. You may also want to place a small cushion or folded bath towel under your buttocks. In any case, be sure to loosen any tight clothing and take off your shoes.

How Much Massage?

I suggest aiming for three approximately ten-minute massage sessions a day, at least one of which amounts to a basic, complete treatment as described in the next chapter. The other sessions may include foot, hand, ear, and *hara* (abdominal) massage, along with diagnostic procedures and exercises suited to your child's age. Many exercises, as well as the treatments in chapter 9, are designed for occasional use when the opportunity, or the need, arises.

But don't worry if you can't manage to achieve this goal on a regular basis. Remember that it is up to your baby to decide how long any massage session lasts. Also, the sessions should be pleasant interludes for you—a way of playing with and feeling close to your child. However, do try to stimulate all the meridians at least once daily. In chapter 5 you will find some shortcuts to accomplishing this on the days when you just cannot fit in an unhurried full massage.

4 · Giving a Basic, Complete Massage

The procedures for a complete massage described and pictured in this chapter can be started as soon as your baby's navel is entirely healed. Once you are familiar with them, you can give your infant a basic treatment that adequately stimulates all fourteen meridians in as little as five to ten minutes. Thus playtime before or after a bath or during a diaper change can become the occasion for a health-promoting shiatsu session. Aim for three of these a day.

Learning the Knack

I suggest that you read through this entire chapter quickly before starting to memorize how to give a complete massage. Fundamentally, all you have to learn is in which direction to stroke the back, front, and sides of your child's body and limbs, so that you move down yang meridians and up yin ones.

There is a trick for getting the hang of this. Look at the illustrations on pages 6 and 7 of the yang and yin meridians. From these illustrations you can see why shiatsu teachers often say that the back of the body is yang, the front yin—with the sole exception of the stomach meridian, which, though yang, is located on the front or yin side of the body and runs down the torso and legs (page 8). Keep this helpful generalization in mind. In addition, you will need to remember that your baby's sides and the outsides of his legs are yang, while the inside of the legs is yin. Finally, remember that when stroking your baby's arms, you must always imagine them to be raised straight up overhead, as in the illustrations on pages 6 and 7. This reminds you to move from wrist to shoulder on the back of the arms (yang) and from armpit to wrist on the palm side (yin). With these tips, you should soon learn to give a basic massage without needing to look at this book.

Position and Technique

You can give your massage either standing, with your baby in front of you on a changing table, or sitting on the floor in any fashion that suits you. One of my favorite positions for massaging my son when he was a baby was to sit on the floor with my legs stretched straight out in front of me and nestle him between them, with his feet against my abdomen, or hara, as shown on page 95. This is the position traditionally used by mothers in India and is an especially good way to keep a secure hold on your baby when giving an oil massage. The illustrations here and in following chapters show a variety of other positions in which you can sit.

It is not necessary to trace the meridians in precisely the order pictured here. As your baby gets older and more active, don't try to make him stay put for his massage. Just follow his lead. If he wants to flip from his tummy onto his back before you've finished massaging all the back meridians, go along with him. Switch to meridians that you can reach in the new positions he moves into. He'll expose his backside to you again soon enough.

The pictures suggest a few imaginative ways to reach various meridians when your baby is not in an "orthodox" position for having them massaged. You will probably discover many more on your own. You will also probably find that, after going through an active phase in the latter half of the first year, your child will begin to view massage time as a time when he likes to lie still.

When giving a complete massage, always support or hold your baby gently in some fashion with one hand while stroking with the other. This is in accordance with the traditional shiatsu principle that "one hand remains still while the other moves." Keep at least one hand on your baby throughout the entire massage to ensure continuous touching—and also for safety's sake if he's on a table.

I show five techniques here for giving a complete massage. Each provides a slightly different sensory experience for your baby and for you. So try to switch your technique from session to session.

About Oil Massage

You don't have to use oil every time you massage your baby. But when you do, warm the oil ahead of time to body temperature. You can do this by letting the container sit for a while in a pot of hot water or on the cover of a radiator or, in summer, placing it in a sunny spot for five to ten minutes. Test the temperature of the oil as you would that of milk in a baby's bottle, by sprinkling a drop or two on the inside of your wrist.

Never pour oil directly onto your baby. Put some in the palm of your hand and rub your palms together for several seconds.

You may use baby oil or any natural vegetable oil. In India, mustard oil is used, and in the Orient, sesame oil, which has a mild, pleasant smell. Traditionalists use only oil made from just one kind of plant, which might be sesame, corn, or something else—but no mixtures.

Adjusting Your Program As Your Child Grows

On pages 40–51, you will find specific guidelines for adapting the basic massage shown here to suit the needs of older babies and toddlers. Once your child is walking and has a longer attention span, you may want to reduce the number of daily sessions from three to two. One session of about twenty minutes could include exercises along with a complete massage. A shorter ten-minute session, composed of massage only, could be used to calm and relax your child in the late afternoon, or whenever needed. Though babies benefit from an exercise-enriched program as they get older, they do not outgrow the need for a basic complete massage. This serves to relieve tiredness and tension and also teaches them, indirectly, how to relax on their own.

FIVE TECHNIQUES

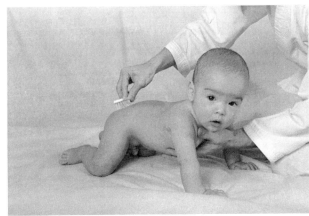

To stroke or rub your baby's meridian lines you can use a soft brush, such as an infant's hairbrush, . . .

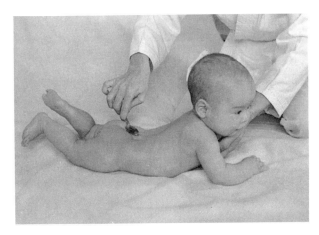

a warm teaspoon, . . .

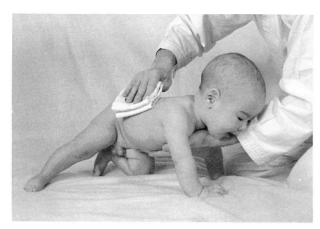

a pad of gauze or cheesecloth
or a folded cotton
handkerchief, . . .

one or two fingers, . . .

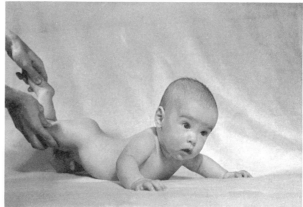

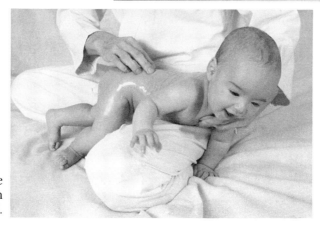

or your whole
hand covered with
warm oil.

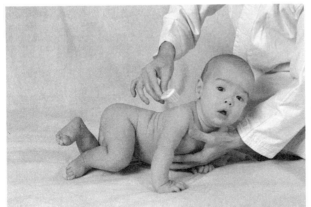

TRACING THE MERIDIANS

With your baby flat on his stomach or in crawling position, stroke down the bladder meridian, inner and outer, from shoulders . . .

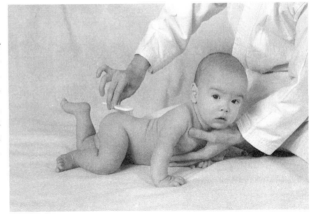

to legs. Do three times on one side of the spine, then repeat on the other side. If you are using a brush, pad, or your hand, you can massage the inner and outer meridian simultaneously, but when using your finger or a spoon, you will need to do each branch separately.

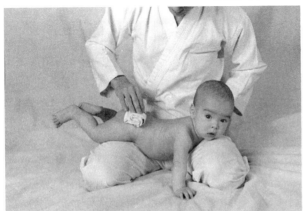

Then stroke down the length of the spine, directly over the backbone (governing vessel meridian), three times.

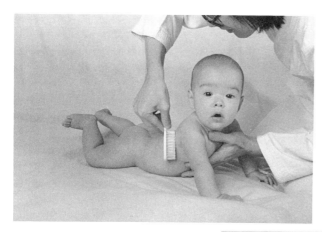

Stroke down the baby's side and the outside edge of his leg (gall bladder meridian) from his armpit . . .

to his ankle. Do three times on each side.

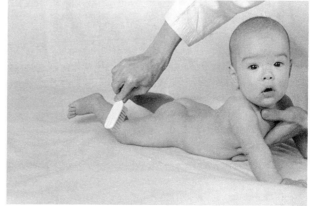

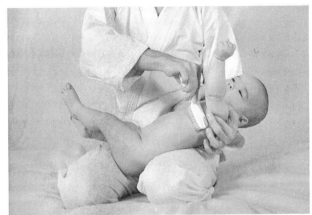

The gall bladder meridian can be stroked with your baby on his back, as well as on his stomach.

Stroke along the back of your baby's arm down the three yang meridians—large intestine, triple heater, and small intestine—from wrist to shoulder. With a brush, pad, or your hand, you can massage all three meridians at once, but when using a spoon or one finger, you may need to stroke each meridian separately. Do each arm three times. Obviously, this routine, too, can be done with your baby on his back.

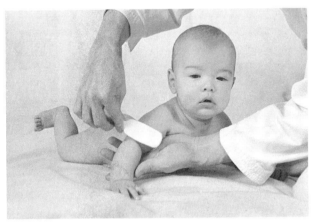

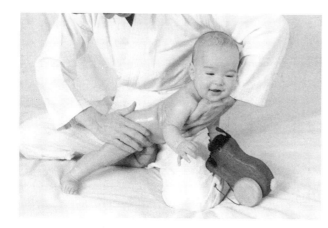

Stroke down the front of each leg (stomach meridian) from hip . . .

to ankle three times. You can reach this meridian with your baby on his side, . . .

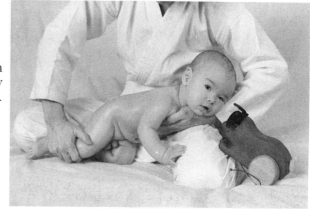

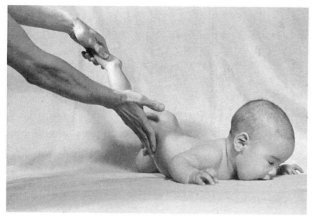

stomach, or back.

With your baby on his back, stroke up the middle of his stomach (conception vessel and kidney meridians) from crotch to neck. Do three times.

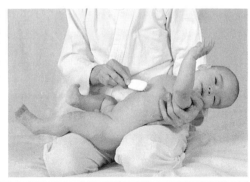

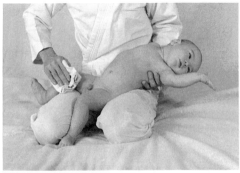

Stroke up the yin meridians on the inside of each leg (spleen, liver, and kidney) from ankle to crotch, three times. Do each meridian individually if you are using a spoon or your finger, but otherwise do all three at once. (Baby may be on his back or stomach.)

Stroke up the yin meridians on the front (palm side) of each arm (lung, heart constrictor, and heart) from armpit to wrist, three times. Even with a spoon or one finger, these three meridians can be done simultaneously. Baby may be on his back or stomach.

After tracing all the meridians, you may want to finish your session by giving some attention to your child's neck and head. This will rejuvenate areas of the body that are especially subject to muscle tension and tiredness, at any age. For the neck area, use the procedure on page 56. Massage the head as shown on pages 93–94.

5 · Foot, Hand, Ear, and Hara Routines

The four kinds of massage shown in this chapter are of special importance for a variety of reasons. Two of them (foot and ear) can be used as alternatives to giving a basic complete massage when you are pressed for time or in a place where it is not feasible to undress your baby. One (hara) is an ancient Oriental procedure for maintaining health, diagnosing, treating ailments, and preventing constitutional problems. All four can be safely used as soon as your infant's navel is fully healed, and they are just as beneficial for an older baby or young child as for a newborn. All deserve a place in your daily massage program.

Foot Massage

According to traditional Oriental thinking, the foot mirrors the entire body, so foot massage promotes health throughout the body. As you can see by looking at the illustrations of the meridians (pages 6–14), many of them either end or begin in the feet. The foot is considered by shiatsu specialists as a "safe area"—that is, you can work on it for as long as you please without danger of overstimulating any meridians or organs.

The foot also tells a great deal about a person's psychology. Orientals believe that the feet reveal more of an individual's real nature than the hands do. When your baby is relaxed and happy, his toes are open and pliant. If he is uncomfortable or anxious for any reason, he curls his toes. Thus his feet are a clue to his inner state. An example is the baby who claps his hands with apparent delight at the sight of visiting Halloween trick-or-treaters, but keeps his toes curled.

The foot massage shown here not only stimulates all of a baby's meridians and organs, but also is good preparation for walking and a good way to relieve tension in the feet and ankles after your child starts to walk. In addition, it is a reliable guide to the condition of your baby's feet and helps prevent foot problems. Healthy feet are warm and their flesh is elastic. All toes rotate smoothly and joints are flexible. There should be no sign of pain when the feet are massaged as instructed. Any obvious deviation from this state of affairs should be discussed with your physician.

Because of the multiple benefits of foot massage, I recommend that you use it regularly from earliest infancy on. This is something you can do while waiting in a doctor's office or, in warm weather, sitting on a park bench with your baby in his carriage.

With your child lying on his back, grasp one of his ankles with one hand, and with the thumb and forefinger of your other hand massage and gently pull each toe. Repeat on the other foot.

Still holding his ankle with one hand, use the thumb of your other hand to press gently and with a jiggling motion for a minute or two on the center of his foot just above the main arch (kidney #1). Repeat on other foot.

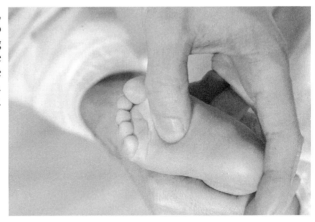

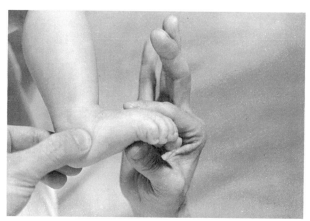

Grasp the back of your child's ankle
with the thumb and forefinger of one
hand and the front of his foot with
your other hand, as shown. While
massaging his ankle between your
thumb and finger, stretch his toes up
gently toward his leg, extending his
Achilles tendon, for a minute or two.
Do both feet.

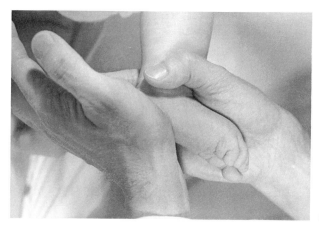

Hold your child's ankle with one
hand, and with the palm of your other
hand massage the sole of his foot by
rubbing your palm back and forth for
a minute or two.

Hand Massage

Since an infant's hands are often in a fist, opening them up, stretching them gently and massaging the palms provide your baby with a novel sensation that is also developmentally beneficial. It is good preparation for crawling and other skills for which opening the hands is necessary.

Hand massage has other uses as well. It helps to maintain good circulation and is a traditional shiatsu technique for calming a nervous or cranky child.

This is another way to massage your baby and young child in public places. When you give hand massage at home, I suggest using warm oil. Afterward, you can wipe off any excess oil with a tissue, so that your baby won't eat it.

Grasp one of your child's hands between your thumb and fingers, as pictured. While gently massaging the center of his palm (heart constrictor #8) with your thumb, use your other hand to uncurl and stretch his fingers, bending them back slightly and . . .

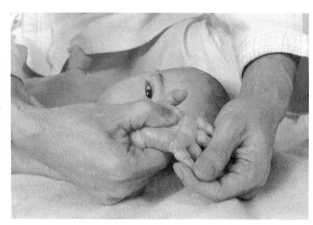

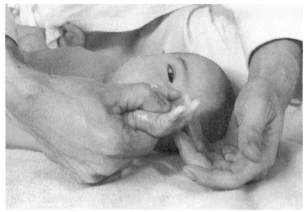

slowly sliding your hand off their tips. Keep doing this for about three minutes on each hand.

Still holding one of your child's palms between your thumb and fingers, use your other hand to stretch each of his fingers individually, sliding each between your thumb and forefinger, from base to tip, three times. Then . . .

finish by massaging the center of his palm (heart constrictor #8) with your thumb for a minute or two. Repeat on other hand.

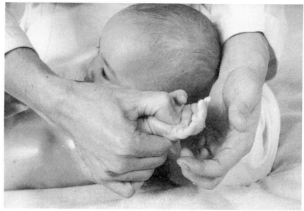

Auricular (Ear) Therapy

In Oriental medicine, the ear is considered one of the most important areas of the body. Like the foot, it mirrors the entire body—its resemblance to a curled-up fetus is often noted. It contains numerous points used by acupuncturists for a wide variety of purposes.

In Eastern folklore big earlobes signify long life, happiness, and good fortune, hence the huge lobes with which the Buddha is always shown. For this reason Oriental parents traditionally pull their children's earlobes regularly. My parents did this with me when I was a boy, in a spirit of fun, much as some people knock on wood. Once, after I was grown, I called them from this country and said kiddingly that thanks to their pulling my ears I was happy and healthy but, unfortunately, not rich. Back came the reply: "Sorry. We forgot to pull both ears."

Joking aside, auricular therapy, like foot massage, stimulates the entire body. But the ear is a more sensitive area than the foot, so massaging it should not be overdone. Once a day is often enough for the auricular therapy shown here, unless you are using it as a treatment to stimulate an underactive child (page 103). Then do it twice a day.

The ear is also a very sensuous structure, as its use by adults in sexual foreplay indicates. The procedures to be described usually make children very happy. They also encourage closeness with parents and healthy sexual development.

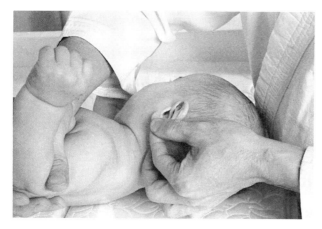

With your child lying on his back, hold one of his arms at the elbow and turn his head to one side, as shown. Grasp his earlobe between the thumb and forefinger of your other hand and slowly slide your fingers down and off the lobe, pulling gently. Do each lobe six times.

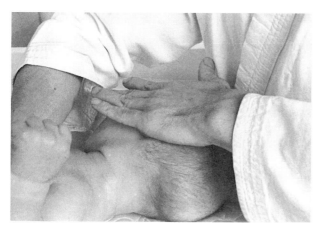

Warm your palms by rubbing them together briskly. With your child in the same position and held as before, place the palm of your free hand over his ear and massage it gently by rubbing first clockwise, then counterclockwise for a minute or two in each direction. Next, press your palm over the center of your baby's ear to form a seal. Hold for several seconds, then slowly slide your hand up over his ear and off the top of his head. Repeat the entire procedure on the other ear.

Caution: Do not suddenly break the seal over your child's ear by removing your palm abruptly, as this might injure his eardrum. Just slide your hand gradually off his ear and head.

Hara Massage

To shiatsu practitioners the hara, or abdomen, is the most vital area of the body. Hara massage is used to promote good health generally and maintain proper functioning of all organs, especially the digestive system. It is also a traditional shiatsu treatment for many common complaints—poor appetite, indigestion, anemia, diarrhea, and constipation—as indicated in chapter 9. I recommend using it regularly during your child's early years to foster a sound constitution in later life. Because the hara is a "private area" not usually touched by outsiders, massaging it also helps build emotional security.

Healthy babies and young children enjoy having their tummies massaged in the way described here. Any sign of discomfort (not to be confused with restlessness) during the procedure should alert you to a possible problem. If you detect a tender area or unusual bulge in the abdominal region, consult your child's doctor.

Hara massage is especially valued in the East as a diagnostic tool. The principles of Eastern hara diagnosis are explained and illustrated in the chapter on diagnostic procedures (page 57).

Warm your hands by rubbing your palms together briskly for a minute or two. Then place both hands side by side on your baby's stomach, or hara, and massage it gently by . . .

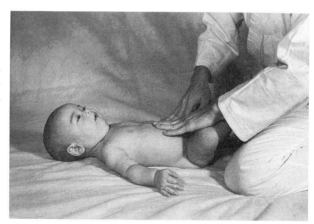

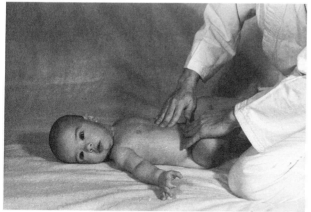

moving your hands clockwise around the entire area for several minutes.

Caution: Always massage the hara clockwise, never in the other direction.

This chapter shows some different ways to stimulate all or a few especially important meridians or parts of the body. These approaches differ from the methods for gentle stroking, demonstrated in chapter 4 on how to give a basic massage, in that they provide more stimulation. Most are modified versions of traditional shiatsu techniques used with adults. However, when using them with older babies and young children, we do not apply the kind of pressure that characterizes shiatsu treatments for mature individuals.

You can start using these alternative techniques after your baby is four months old or is able to lift his head and shoulders and hold them up steadily when in the prone position, whichever comes sooner. Two of the techniques (thumb and tingly) are suitable for giving a complete basic massage. Others are appropriate just for treating specific meridians or body areas. Each is recommended for special purposes, to be pointed out.

Once your baby is old enough, I recommend substituting various alternative techniques for simple stroking during all or part of your child's daily complete massage, at least most of the time. This will afford variety, as well as additional stimulation. However, there will be occasions when stroking alone seems to you to be more appropriate, because of its soothing effect. You are the best judge of your child's needs and moods. Follow your instincts. When you do confine yourself just to stroking throughout a massage, feel free with an older baby to use a somewhat "heavier hand." Also, move along the meridians a bit more slowly.

Role of Bladder Meridian and Back Massage

As you read through this chapter, you will notice that I suggest a number of ways to massage just your child's bladder meridian or back as a whole. The reason is that the bladder meridian is much the longest of all the meridians and contains many "associated points," that is, tsubos that affect some organ or function in addition to the bladder meridian. The drawing on page 39 shows the organs and functions affected when various areas of the back are massaged. As you can see, when you work on your child's back, you give a general internal tune-up. Also, back massage, like hara massage, can provide diagnostic information. With experience, you may learn to detect changes, such as heightened tension or tenderness, that indicate a possible problem with the organ or function associated with the area of the back involved.

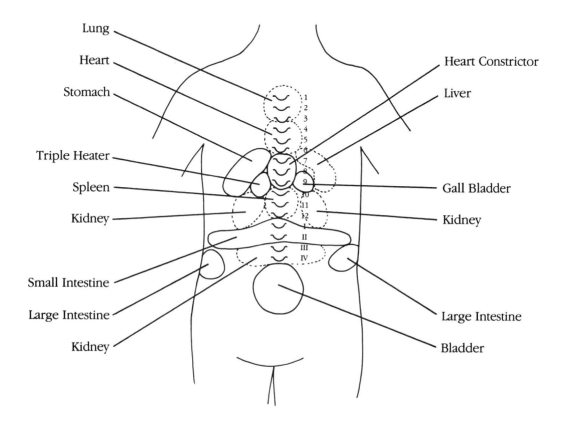

"Map of the Back," showing relation of specific areas of the back to specific organs and functions. Used in shiatsu as a guide to both treating and diagnosing problems.

Fold and Roll

This ancient Oriental technique is designed to develop sensory awareness. It also serves to foster and maintain good circulation and helps protect your child against colds and other respiratory ills.

The technique is not suited to giving a complete massage. Just use it on the meridians indicated, for the purposes named. Before trying it on your baby, practice with one hand on your own arm, or with both hands on an adult's back.

With your child on her stomach, use the thumb and next two fingers of both your hands to pick up a fold of skin over the large muscles on both sides of your child's spine at the shoulders (outer bladder meridian). Then, . . .

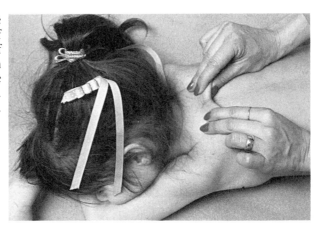

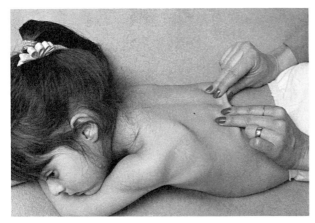

"walk" your thumbs and fingers down your child's back, from shoulders to hips, while gently rolling the fold of skin between them. Do three times.

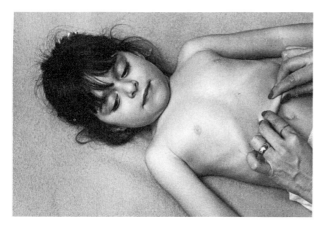

With your child on her back, use the same technique to roll a fold of skin up the middle of her stomach (conception vessel and kidney meridians) from her groin . . .

to her shoulders. Do three times.

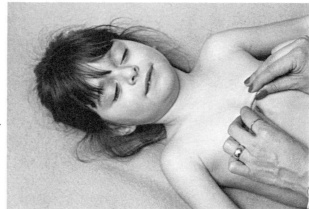

Using Your Thumbs

Though you will press only very lightly when massaging your child this way, the technique illustrated is a modified version of a traditional shiatsu procedure used with adults. As the pictures show, you always work with the ball, never the tip of your thumb. Keep the first joint of your thumb fully extended, to form an arc, and your other fingers relaxed. Even in its modified form, this method provides deeper stimulation than the other techniques described in this book.

Here I demonstrate how to work on your baby's back with both thumbs at once, to promote muscular and locomotive development and prevent spinal distortion. You can give a complete massage with this technique. But when you do, use just *one* thumb at a time during the rest of the massage and hold your child with your other hand, according to the principle stated in chapter 4 that "one hand remains still while the other moves." Also, do not stop and press in the hara area. Merely slide your thumb slowly along the meridians there.

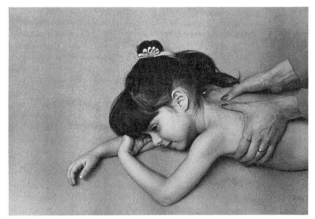

With your child on her stomach, place your thumbs in the grooves on either side of her spine (bladder meridian) and slowly move them down her back from her shoulders . . .

to her buttocks, stopping to press gently every inch or so for several seconds. Do three times. Then, . . .

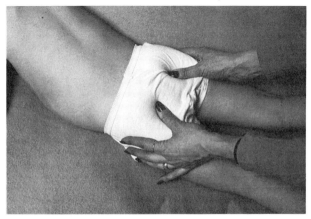

massage the entire buttocks area with your thumbs, moving them around both mounds at the same time for about three minutes.

Tingly Massage

In Japan today the kind of massage to be described is generally performed with a small hand-held instrument consisting of a serrated metal wheel encased between two smooth wheels attached to a short handle. When this instrument is rolled along a meridian, the serrated wheel makes enough contact with the skin to produce a slight tingling, but leaves no mark. A student describes the sensation as a "tickle with a zing." Since this instrument is not available in the West, to massage your child this way, you will have to use what the Japanese used in earlier times: your fingernails (well trimmed and smoothed, of course).

To get an idea of how this feels and how much pressure to use, run your nails up the inside of your own bare arm. Then test the technique on your baby's bare back.

The pictures here show the treatment being used just on the inner bladder meridian on the back, primarily for the purpose of stimulating the autonomic nervous system, which controls involuntary body functions such as breathing, heartbeat, and intestinal flow. However, you can give a complete basic massage this way, provided that keeping your fingers bent is not overtiring for you. A tingly massage gives extra stimulation to the meridians.

With your child on her stomach, place one of your hands at the base of her skull, as shown, exerting slight pressure upward. With the nails of the first two fingers of your other hand, stroke down the grooves on both sides of her spine (bladder meridian) from her shoulders . . .

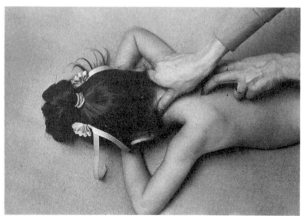

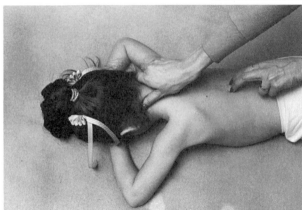

to the end of her spine. Do this twice. Then . . .

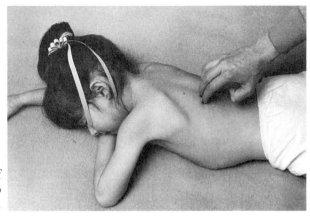

do two more times, using the nails of four fingers, two on one side and two on the other side of her spine.

Two Ways to Enliven a Diaper Change

Both these procedures for back massage are easier to carry out when you are standing, with your baby on a changing table. Therefore, I recommend using them during the course of a diaper change. They are fun and provide a lot of stimulation quickly.

The first, using your forearm, is another traditional shiatsu technique modified for use with babies and young children. Note that you keep your hand bent back at the wrist, with your palm and fingers relaxed, so that the muscles of your forearm are relatively soft.

The second is a general massage technique used all over the world to stimulate a large area of the body in a short amount of time. In this instance, you ignore the direction of the energy flow in the meridians.

With your baby on his stomach, facing you, place your left hand under his chest (right hand, if you are left-handed) to hold him as shown. With your other forearm stroke down his back, from his shoulders to his ankles, on first one side, then the other. Do each side, alternately, three times. Try to maintain a nice, continuous, sweeping motion. You will be massaging the governing vessel, bladder, and gall bladder meridians.

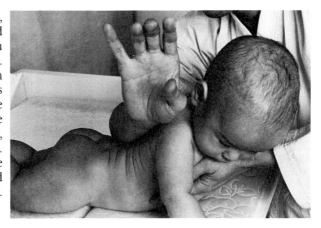

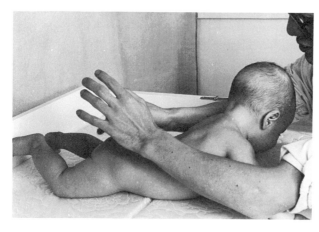

With your baby in the same position, use both hands to stroke rhythmically first down, . . .

then up the entire back area (same meridians as before). Do this half a dozen times or more, moving your body forward and back from your hips as you stroke.

Caution: Your baby's feet should point toward the wall against which the changing table is placed, so that he can't fall off in that direction. Your body and arms protect him from the front and sides.

Three Routines When Sitting Western Style

Contrary to what my students may think, I do sometimes sit
Western style—on chairs. The three routines for back massage
shown here are for use in that position.

The first two are a playful way to stimulate the bladder meridian.
Babies and young children find the rhythm of the activity highly
enjoyable.

The third routine is valuable because it can be done anywhere,
even when you are riding in a bus with your child. Though the
baby pictured here has no clothes on, you need not undress your
child for this procedure. Besides stimulating the bladder meridian,
it is a traditional Oriental remedy for crankiness, upset stomach,
and hiccups. I also recommend it as a good way to burp your baby.

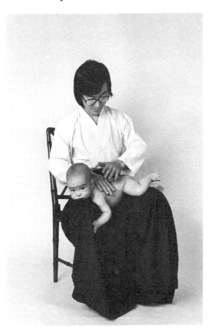

With your baby lying on his stomach across your lap,
rub down the entire width of his back, from shoulders
to thighs, with first one hand, then the other. Only one
hand should be on your child at any given instant.
Stroke for two or three minutes, speeding up the action
gradually.

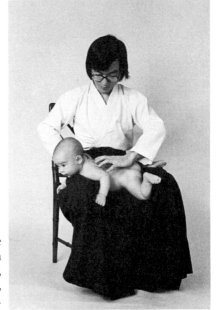

This is a variation of the preceding routine. In the same
position, run your fingernails lightly down both
sides of your child's spine (bladder meridian),
using first one hand, then the other, as before,
and speeding up gradually.

Hold your baby with one arm, as shown, with his
buttocks resting on your hand and his head on your
shoulder. His body should slant downward evenly from
his head to his rump. Rock him in this position for
several minutes. Then, . . . while continuing to rock, use
your free hand to stroke down his entire back area from
his shoulders to his thighs. Stroke three or more times.

Kenbiki Back Massage

Kenbiki, which means "pushing and pulling muscles," is a traditional shiatsu technique for relieving tension in various parts of the body. You use your thumb and fingers to grasp and knead muscled areas—in the way you would knead the back of your calf if you got a cramp there.

Of course, when you use kenbiki on a baby's or young child's back, you grasp and knead very gently. Still, you move the flesh and muscles around to a greater extent than is possible with other techniques in this book. In the process, you stimulate the back meridians (and associated organs and functions) and also leave the entire back area relaxed and free of tension. Babies love it.

This is another procedure for which you need not undress your child. So you can use it any time you are holding him—while walking, standing in the checkout line at your supermarket, waiting for a bus, and so on. It is also a sophisticated way to burp your baby. When using kenbiki for burping, devote special attention to the part of your child's back known to shiatsu practitioners as the "stomach area" (illustration on page 39).

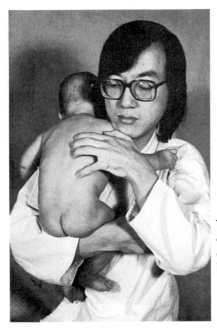

While holding your child against your shoulder with one arm, as shown, use your other hand to give kenbiki down the big muscles at either side of the spine (outer bladder meridian) from shoulder . . .

to buttocks. Do each side three times. Then . . .

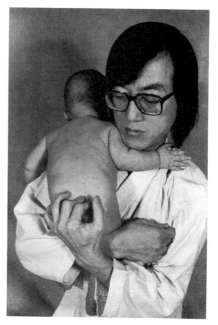

knead both buttocks simultaneously with your thumb and fingers, as pictured, for a minute or two.

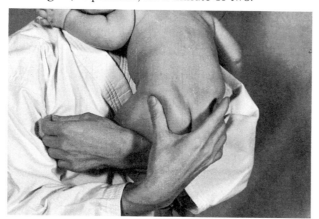

You have already been introduced to some shiatsu techniques that give you diagnostic information. To the skilled shiatsu practitioner, every procedure is a source of such information. Conversely, almost no routines are used solely for diagnosis. Of the six procedures covered in this chapter, all but one provide various other benefits, to be pointed out, besides functioning as diagnostic tools.

About Oriental Diagnosis

The word "diagnosis" has a broader meaning in traditional Oriental medicine than it has in Western medical practice. It is not just a matter of finding out what is wrong with an individual who is obviously sick. It also involves detecting potential problems, ones that may not yet be apparent to Western eyes. Since it often reveals conditions that are not yet serious and will correct themselves with just the aid of natural measures such as proper diet, exercise, or massage, it is a potent preventive health measure.

The subtlety of Oriental diagnosis is particularly relevant in the case of babies. Accurately evaluating their physical status is especially hard, because their bodies are so small, they can't talk, and their condition can change drastically in a very short time.

There are many Oriental proverbs about the skill needed to determine a baby's condition. One goes: "An average doctor can diagnose and cure a grown male; it takes a better doctor to diagnose and cure a grown female; only the best doctor can diagnose and cure a baby." Another proverb pays tribute to the insights gained through parental experience: "The mother of three healthy children is more of an expert on infant health than the best doctor."

When you use shiatsu for diagnosing, you are also treating, and vice versa. Your hands alert you to anything that might lead to trouble, and, at the same time, they help to ward it off. That's the holistic approach to health.

The six procedures shown here offer a way to keep track of your child's health from day to day. All six can be safely used as soon as your baby's navel is healed. By using them regularly, you will become able to spot subtle changes in your offspring's condition that call for an alteration in everyday care. You will also be alerted early to any structural or other problems that need to be brought to a doctor's attention. This chapter should help you become a better judge of when to consult your doctor, what to say, and how to work more knowledgeably with medical personnel.

Fontanel Diagnosis

Parents are often unnecessarily afraid to touch their baby's fontanel, or "soft spot"—the area on top of the head where the bones have not yet grown together, which is covered by a tough membrane. You can't harm your infant by touching this spot lightly, as directed here. Medical personnel do. And the area is frequently subjected to rougher contact (also harmless) due to a baby's own movements.

This procedure is the only one used solely for diagnostic purposes. It is a simple, effective way to gauge the state of your baby's health until the fontanel eventually closes, sometime between about nine months and two years. If you do it several times a day, you will soon become an expert at recognizing any variations from normal that should be watched. Variations to look for and their significance are:

1) If the fontanel pulse is irregular or unusually strong or weak, the baby may be contracting an illness. Be alert for other indications that he needs special attention from you or his doctor.

2) If the membrane over the area seems concave (sunk below the surface), dehydration is indicated. The baby needs to get or retain more fluid. This can help you keep track of the seriousness of diarrhea. If, on the other hand, the membrane appears convex (protrudes noticeably) the baby is getting or retaining too much fluid, possibly due to overfeeding. If either condition continues for long (more than three or four hours), consult your doctor.

3) If the area feels hot, the baby is sleepy, hungry, or coming down with a fever. Common sense will usually tell you which.

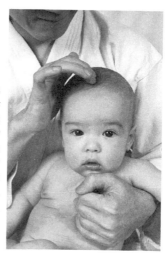

Rest two fingers of one hand lightly on your baby's fontanel for about thirty seconds and observe the quality of the pulse and condition of the membrane that covers the spot. In a well baby, the pulse is regular and easily discernible, but not extremely strong. The membrane forms a taut, even surface; it neither sinks in nor protrudes obviously. After you have checked the pulse and membrane on a dozen or so occasions, you will develop a sure feel for what is their usual, or normal, condition, and what isn't.

Judging Spinal Alignment

When a child is lying stretched out straight on his stomach, his spine normally curves smoothly along its length, as shown in the following drawing, but is not bent to either side. Daily use of the procedure demonstrated here will develop your ability to pick up any variations from normal alignment, which should be discussed with your doctor. For treatment of minor distortions, see pages 42–43, 56, 61, 81, and 100–101.

This routine also stimulates the governing vessel meridian, which, along with the bladder meridian, controls the autonomic nervous system. Therefore, it is traditionally used in the East to promote the development of this nervous system, as well as for diagnosis.

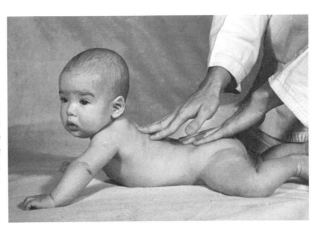

Be sure your hands are warm. With your child lying on his stomach, use both hands, one placed beneath and just below the other, as shown, to stroke gently down the spine (governing vessel meridian) from shoulders . . .

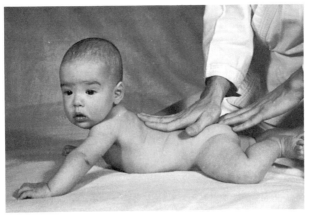

to hips. Repeat several times. Use warm baby oil on your hands if you like.

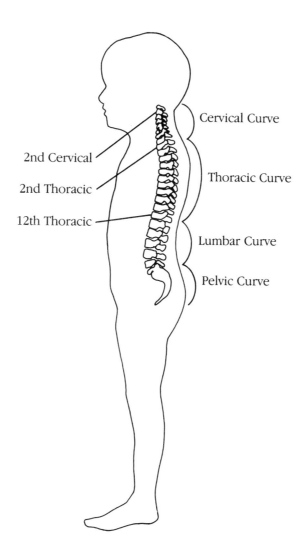

2nd Cervical

2nd Thoracic

12th Thoracic

Cervical Curve

Thoracic Curve

Lumbar Curve

Pelvic Curve

Normal curve of the spine along its length, as seen from the side. Any marked deviation from this, or bend to either side, should be discussed with your doctor.

Checking Neck, Shoulders, and Spine

This procedure is both a diagnostic tool and an exercise. As a diagnostic tool, it offers another way to judge the condition of the spine, plus a check on neck and shoulder development. When rotating your child's head as illustrated, notice whether it moves with equal ease to each side. Even movement in both directions indicates healthy development of the spine, the neck, and shoulder muscles. If the head obviously moves less easily to one side than the other, bring this to the attention of your doctor.

As an exercise, this routine, used regularly, helps to foster good spinal alignment and good development of the neck and shoulders. It is also an excellent way to relax these structures in any young child, but especially after a baby has been sitting up or propped in a sitting position for some time.

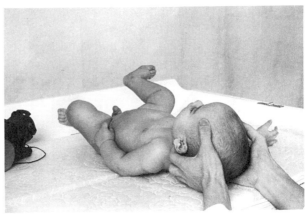

With your child lying on his back, cradle his head in your hands as shown, with your fingers on the sides and back of his neck and your thumbs at his temples.

Gently rotate his head to one side, then the other, lifting it slightly as you rotate, so that it moves up, over, and down in a smooth arc. Go several times to each side. Move your entire upper body, not just your hands and arms, when doing this.

Hara Diagnosis

Because of the special value of hara massage for therapeutic purposes, it was included in an earlier chapter (page 36). The technique described here is slightly different from that recommended earlier as a treatment, but you can combine the two methods, and diagnose as you treat.

A healthy child has a nicely elastic hara. When your child is lying on his back and relaxed, the area should be very soft. When he is laughing, crying, or eliminating, the area should become quite hard. An abdomen that protrudes when a child is lying supine, yet shows no muscular strength, indicates a digestive problem, either temporary or longer lasting.

As you grow accustomed to how your child's hara normally feels when you massage it, you may become sensitive to subtle signals. Are there portions of the abdomen that seem less relaxed and yielding to the touch than the region as a whole? In Eastern diagnosis, such spots are viewed as clues to organs or body functions that are less healthy than they could be. The drawing on page 59 shows the relation between specific areas of the hara and specific organs and functions.

Once you are aware of these clues to your child's health, you can usually prevent serious difficulties through the use of natural measures—shiatsu and proper diet. However, if you have any other reason to suspect an organic or functional problem, consult your doctor. The earlier a problem is detected, the easier it is to cure.

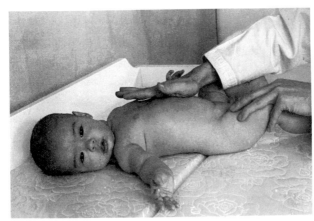

Be sure your hands are warm. With your child lying on his back, grasp one of his knees in one hand and with the palm of your other hand gently rub clockwise around the entire hara area for several minutes. Then, . . .

do the same thing using your fingertips. Finally, . . .

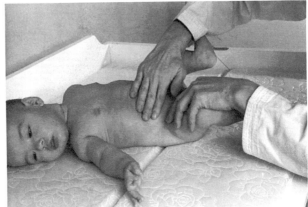

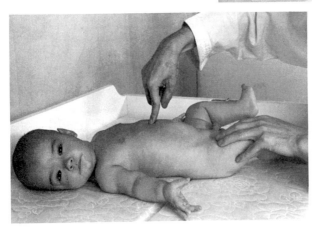

Repeat with just your forefinger. Use oil for this procedure if you wish.

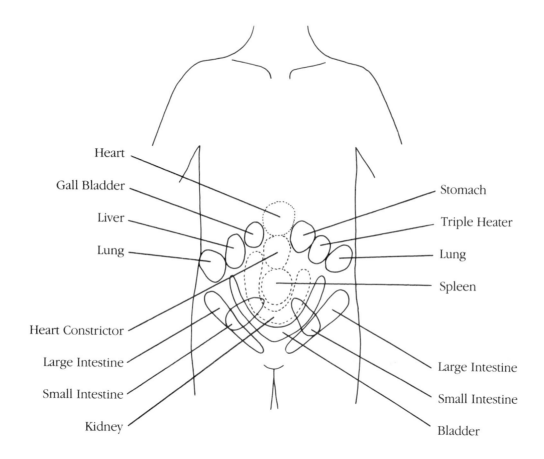

Heart
Gall Bladder
Liver
Lung

Stomach
Triple Heater
Lung
Spleen

Heart Constrictor
Large Intestine
Small Intestine
Kidney

Large Intestine
Small Intestine
Bladder

The relation of specific areas of the
hara to specific organs and functions.
Unusual tension or stiffness in any of
these areas suggests weakness of the
organ or function associated with it.

Checking the Cranium

A healthy cranium curves smoothly all over, with no decidedly flat spots along the sides or back, and with its left and right halves symmetrically developed. The procedure here is a way to tell whether your baby's skull is developing evenly, make sure he is not sleeping too much in one position, and check the condition of the skull after a fall. Any marked unevenness detected at any time should be brought to the attention of your doctor.

The procedure is also useful for treatment purposes. After a difficult delivery, this kind of gentle head shiatsu, done regularly, is a way to help a baby's cranium acquire a good shape. It encourages the growth of hair, helps to relieve the pain of minor mishaps, and contributes to feelings of security, so try it when your child is upset, cranky, or fearful.

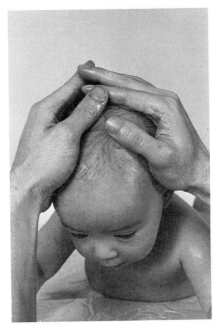

Warm your hands by rubbing them together briskly for a minute or two. With your baby on his stomach, facing you, use both hands to rub down his head gently from the top of his skull to his chin. Do four or five times.

Hip-Joint Diagnosis

This is both a diagnostic tool for detecting hip-joint problems and an exercise that helps prevent them and the spinal difficulties that they may lead to later on. It also provides good preparation for walking.

In doing this procedure, you never use pressure, just guide your child's knees as far in the directions indicated as they go easily. You should feel as if your child were moving his legs on his own. Stop if you encounter any resistance or sign of discomfort.

Consult your doctor about the possibility of a hip-joint problem if you detect any of the following conditions:

1) Your child's knees do not move up evenly, and with equal ease, against his chest and mirror each other's position there.

2) His bent knees do not open out to his sides with equal ease.

3) One or both bent knees do not touch the floor when they are opened out to his sides.

4) His hip joints do not appear to be aligned horizontally when his heels are side by side.

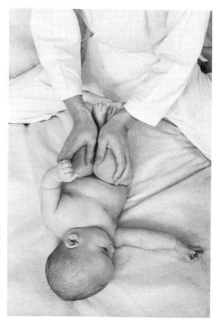

With your child lying on his back, grasp his knees in your hands and gently guide them up against his chest, as shown. Do several times, watching to see if both knees move with equal ease against his chest and line up evenly there. Then, . . .

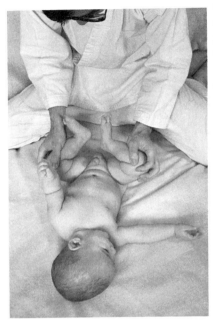

with his knees partially bent and slightly below his hips, as shown, gradually open them out to the sides, checking whether they will touch the floor. *Do not exert pressure, just guide.* Do three times. Next, . . .

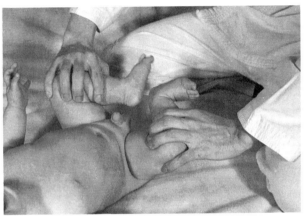

with his knees slightly apart, as shown, flex first one leg, then the other, as if he were bicycling or taking steps, for several minutes. Finally, . . .

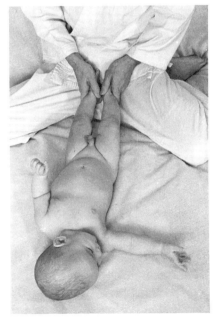

slide your hands down to your baby's ankles, gently stretching his legs out straight, and check whether his hip joints seem to be aligned horizontally with each other when his heels are side by side. Do several times.

Caution: Never apply pressure. Stop if you encounter any resistance or sign of discomfort.

8 · Shiatsu Exercises for Fun and Development

The activities here are ways to have fun with your child that, coincidentally, maximize the developmental benefits of physical play for babies and young children. These are not traditional shiatsu or Japanese activities. I worked them out in the course of playing with my son. However, they all incorporate traditional shiatsu principles. Often, too, as you will recognize, they reflect ways in which parents around the world have traditionally played with their babies and young children.

Shiatsu exercises, like shiatsu massage, are designed to stimulate the meridians, through stretching and other means, and foster a balanced flow of energy throughout the body. Thus they help to maintain general health and ward off sickness. They also promote sound structural development and contribute to a good sense of balance, in which control of bodily movements is centered in the hara. In addition, many that I have devised and demonstrate here provide other special benefits, to be pointed out.

The exercises are divided into three categories: Stretching Routines, Acrobatics, and Hijinks in a Chair. Though nearly all involve stretching various meridians in some way, the categories indicate the activity level of the routines or where you do them.

You can safely begin any of these routines as soon as your baby can raise his head and shoulders and hold them up steadily when in the prone position. After your child matures to this point, I recommend devoting at least ten minutes a day to this kind of active play—more, if convenient. I have purposely included a great many routines so that you can be choosy and switch off. Some provide substitute ways to stimulate specific meridians and may be incorporated into your regular massage program.

A few of these activities will be outgrown within your baby's first year or so. Obviously, for example, your child will not want (or need) to play at standing up, walking, and sitting down once he's mastered these arts. But most routines here continue to be appealing and useful to children into their third year. Use your common sense and knowledge of your own child to decide which are most appropriate at various growth stages. Above all, keep it fun.

STRETCHING ROUTINES

What To Do: With your child on his back, let him grab your thumbs. Close your hands loosely around his fists. Then, . . .

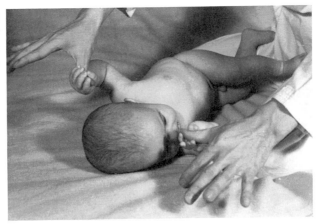

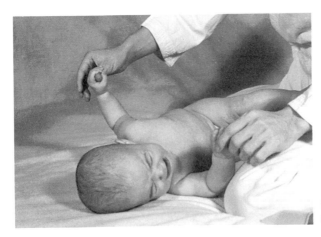

as he inhales, stretch his arms straight out, opening his rib cage. As . . .

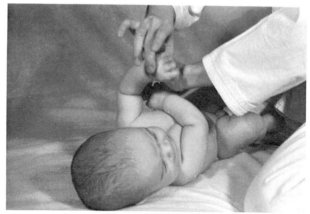

he exhales, cross his arms snugly over his chest, to close the rib cage. Continue about three minutes.

Why? Promotes healthy lung development and helps prevent colds and other respiratory ills. Also good for shoulder and arm development.

Caution: A young baby will release your thumbs if he does not want to do this for any reason. Stop if he does so.

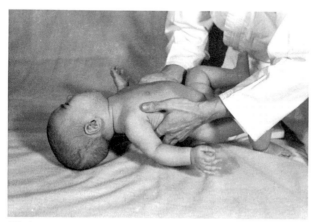

What To Do: With your child on his back, place four fingers of each hand under him just below his armpits, as shown, and lift his torso up a few inches. Then, let his body slide between your hands back onto the floor or changing table. Do three or four times.

Why? Stretches all the muscles and meridians in the torso and encourages free movement of the arms and legs. Especially useful after a baby has been confined for considerable time in a carriage or carrier.

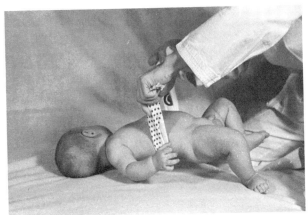

What To Do: Fold a scarf to make a strap two or three inches wide. With your child on his back, use the scarf to lift up his torso a few inches and . . .

tilt him first to one side, . . .

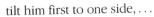

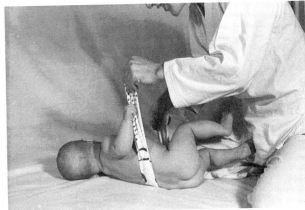

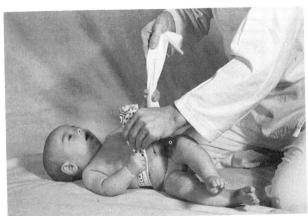

then the other side. Repeat three or four times.

Why? Same as for preceding exercise. In addition, this variant fosters the development of handedness and encourages cross-patterned crawling, in which the hand on one side of the body is advanced in unison with the knee on the other side.

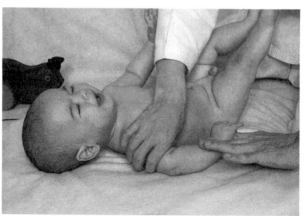

What To Do: With your child on his back, let him grasp your left forefinger in his right hand. Place your other hand at his right armpit, as shown. Gently stretch his right arm out straight, then . . .

rotate it up over his head, across his chest, and down to his side. Do three times, then repeat with the other arm.

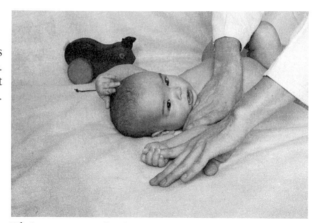

Why? Encourages healthy development of the shoulders and arm sockets. This is also a diagnostic procedure. If one arm rotates much less freely than the other, or if your child suddenly cries during this procedure, check with your doctor about the possibility of an arm-socket problem.

Caution: Stop if your child shows discomfort or, in the case of a baby, releases your finger.

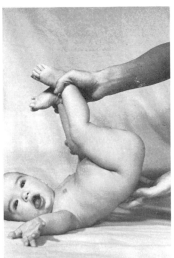

What To Do: With your child on his back, grasp his ankles with one hand, as for diapering, and bounce him playfully on his bottom a couple of times. Then, . . .

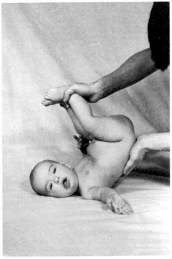

hold him up with only his head and shoulders touching the floor or changing table, and with the fingers of your other hand stroke down the grooves on each side of his spine (bladder meridian), from his shoulders . . .

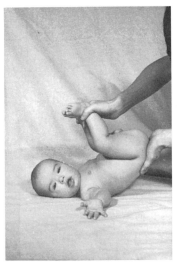

to his hips, while gradually lowering his body. Do three times. Then stroke down the meridian with your fingernails—tingly massage—three more times.

Why? An easy way to massage the bladder meridian of an active baby and, at the same time, stretch the spine and legs. The extra stimulation provided by tingly massage aids the development of the autonomic nervous system.

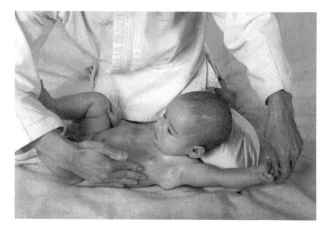

What To Do: With your child on his back, let him grab your thumb, as shown, and, holding his fist loosely, stretch his arm straight up over his head. With the fingers of your other hand, stroke down the side of his body (gall bladder meridian) from his armpit . . .

to his groin, stretching the upper side of his body. Do three times, then repeat on the other side. Use oil if you like.

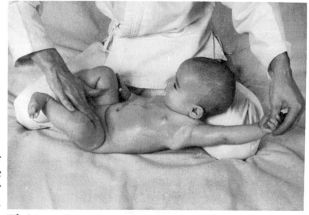

Why? Stimulates the gall bladder meridian through stretching, as well as stroking. Also helps prevent rash under the arms and is good preparation for the "reaching out" involved in crawling.

What To Do: In the same position, place your hands one on top of the other on one side of your child's body at his waist. Slowly . . .

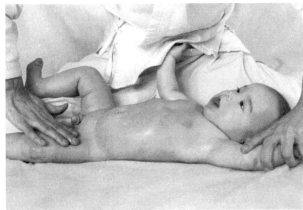

move your hands away from each other along his torso and limbs, stretching gently. When you reach his ankle and wrist, . . .

grasp them and hold his arm and leg out straight briefly before sliding your hands off. Do three times, then repeat on the other side.

Why? Excellent for stretching the sides and limbs and stimulating all meridians there. Promotes good circulation in the extremities—use if your child has a tendency to cold hands and feet.

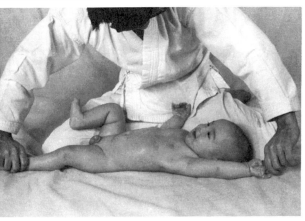

What To Do: With your child on his back, place your right hand on his chest near his right armpit to hold his shoulders down. Put your left hand under his right hip and twist his hip and lower torso up, swinging his right leg over the left one. Keep your hand on his hip, stretching his torso, for several seconds, then return his hip and leg to their original position. Do this three times. Next, . . .

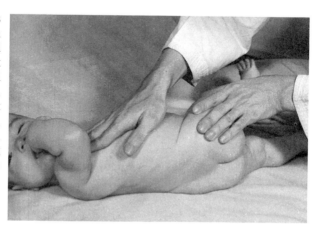

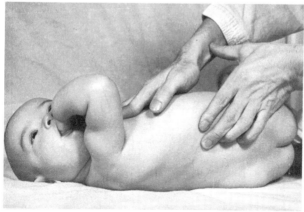

while holding his shoulders on the floor as before, swing him into the same position by stroking down the side of his back (outer bladder meridian) from his shoulder to his hip. Hold as previously, then return to original position. Do three times, then repeat the entire procedure on the other side.

Why? The twisting and stretching stimulates all meridians in the back and relieves muscle tension there.

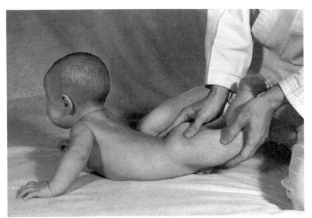

What To Do: With your child on his stomach, place one hand on his buttock and the other under his knee on the same side, as shown. Gently rock his bent leg up toward his head two or three times. Then rub your hand down the back, front, and outside of his thigh (bladder, gall bladder, and stomach meridians) three times. Repeat entire procedure on the other leg.

Why? Contributes to good muscle tone in the legs and prepares them for crawling and walking. Alleviates (or prevents) excessive tiredness in the lower half of the body after a child starts crawling and walking. Relieves (or prevents) diaper rash by stretching the creases in the groin area. This is also another way to check on hip-joint functioning (page 61). Both legs should move up toward the head with equal ease.

Caution: Do not force the upward movement.

What To Do: Kneel Japanese fashion, as shown, with your child on his back across your thighs. Place one hand at his armpit and the other on the same side of his body at the groin. Slowly slide your hands apart to his wrist and ankle, stretching the entire side of his body. Do three times, then repeat on the other side.

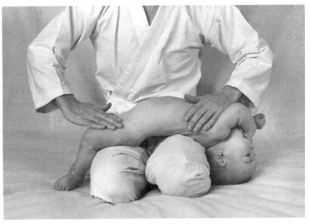

Why? Stretches all the yin meridians and promotes good circulation throughout the body. Also fosters the development of a balanced body structure and is good preparation for walking.

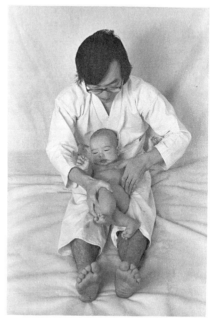

What To Do: Sit on the floor with your legs straight out in front of you. Place your child on his back on your outstretched legs, with his head against your hara. Grasp one of his knees in your hand and cross his leg over the other one. While . . .

gently stretching the leg you are holding, with the palm of your other hand stroke down the side of the leg (gall bladder meridian) from his buttocks to his ankle. Do three times, then repeat on the other leg.

Why? Stimulates all meridians in the leg, as well as gall bladder functioning. Good for relieving the fatigue of walking.

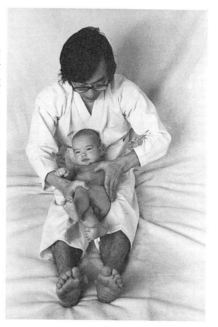

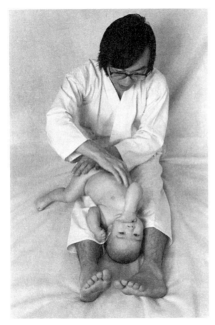

What To Do: Sitting as before, place your child on his back with his head toward your feet and resting on the floor, as shown. Cross one of his legs over the other, turning his lower torso so that his buttocks are perpendicular to the floor. Place one hand on his thigh, and with the fingers of your other hand stroke down his side (gall bladder meridian) from his armpit to his hip, three times. Repeat on the other side.

Why? Fosters flexibility of the torso and stimulates gall bladder functioning.

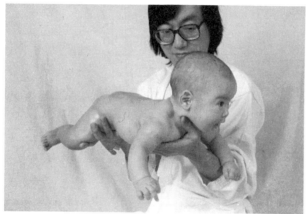

ACROBATICS

What To Do: Hold your child up in the air, slightly away from your body, in the prone position, as shown, with one of your hands under his chest and around his arm and your other hand under his hips and around his leg.

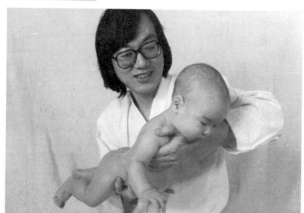

Swing him to one side, . . .

then the other, continuing rhythmically for a few minutes.

Why? Children love this, and it helps develop physical agility and self-confidence. It also helps compensate for time spent in a confined area.

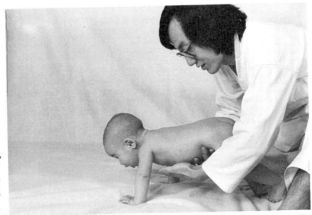

What To Do: With your baby on his stomach on the floor, lift his torso and legs up as shown, so that his arms are straight and support his head and shoulders. Then, . . .

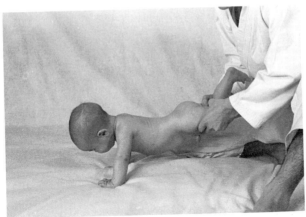

holding his legs at the thighs, encourage him to walk on his hands. When he puts his right hand forward, move his left knee forward and place it on the floor, as for cross-patterned crawling. When he reaches ahead with his left hand, put his right knee forward. Continue for several minutes, or as long as your baby is interested. (Older children who have mastered cross-patterned crawling enjoy walking on their hands while you hold their legs up in the air wheelbarrow fashion.)

Why? Cross-patterned crawling is very important to intellectual development, as well as healthy structural development and good physical coordination. Many children do not automatically crawl this way. To make it second nature, they need playful encouragement, as suggested here and on pages 66 and 80. (Wheelbarrow walking with older children develops stomach muscles.)

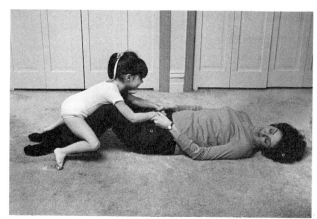

What To Do: Sit or lie on the floor with your child lying face down on your lower legs. Grasp her securely as shown. Slowly . . .

raise your knees and feet so that her body is parallel to the floor. Hold a few seconds. Then . . .

rock her for several minutes, first by raising and lowering your feet, . . .

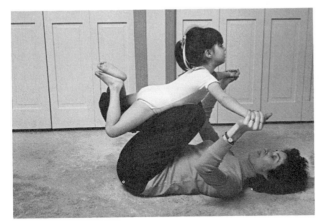

then by moving your knees toward your head and back again. Finally, . . .

let your child grasp your thumbs, hold her fists loosely, stretch her arms out, as for a swan dive, and rock as before.

Why? Promotes balancing ability and self-confidence. For babies, it's good preparation for walking. Nice exercise for parents, too.

Caution: Stop if your child seems uneasy or, in the case of a baby, releases your thumbs. Try again another day.

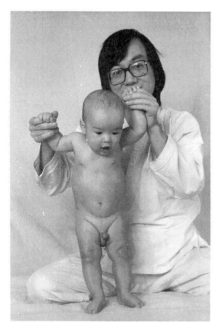

What To Do: While sitting on the floor lotus style, with your baby on your lap, hold his hands and help him pull himself up into a standing position, . . .

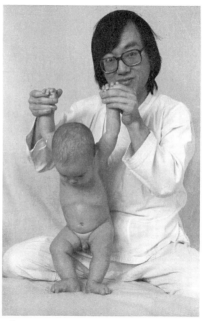

then lower himself back down on his rump. Continue for as long as your baby is interested.

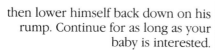

Why? Prepares your baby for walking by helping him master the trick of pulling himself up and getting back down—the latter is harder for many babies.

What To Do: In the same position, let your baby grab your thumbs, then close your hands around his fists and help him stand. Stretch his arms up straight a couple of times. You may lift him completely off the floor if he likes this. Then, . . .

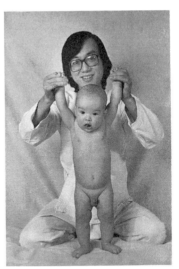

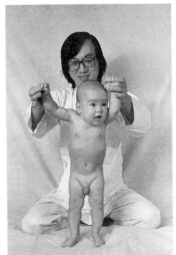

let him step away from you as you support him. To encourage cross-patterning, move his left arm forward as he steps out on his right foot, and his right arm with the left foot, rhythmically. When he has gone as far as you can reach, . . .

turn him around and let him step toward you.

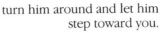

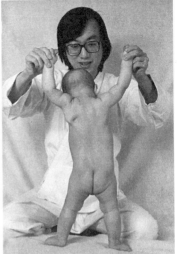

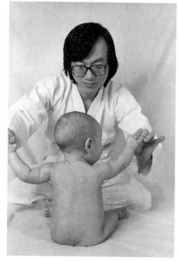

He will release your thumbs or just sit down when he's had enough.

Why? Babies love to practice walking. If you do this with them while sitting on the floor, it's easier on your back, easy to encourage cross-patterning, and allows your baby to feel more in control of the activity.

What To Do: Hold your child upside down by his ankles and gently swing him back and forth a few times.

Why? Healthy children really go for this (usually), and it contributes to good development of the neck, spinal, and hip-joint structures.

Caution: Stop if your child cries. Though crying by itself does not always indicate a structural problem with the neck, spine, or hip joints, consult your doctor about the possibility of such a problem before trying this procedure again.

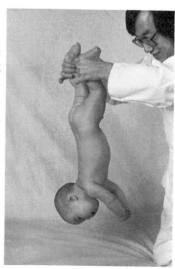

HIJINKS IN A CHAIR

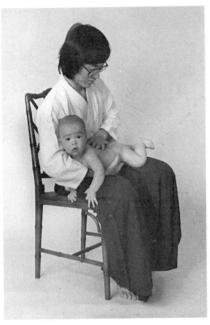

What To Do: While sitting in a straight chair, hold your child across your lap with one arm underneath his body, as shown. Place your other hand on his back, raise him up off your lap and slightly away from your body, and rock him back and forth a few times. Then, . . .

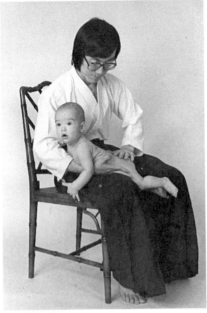

return him to your lap and with your free hand rub down one side of his back and the back of one leg (bladder meridian) all the way from his neck to his ankle. Do each side three times.

Why? Rocking appeals to children and helps cultivate a sense of rhythm and balance, especially if done to music or if you sing to your child. Since the bladder meridian includes so many associated points, when you rub down its entire length, you approximate a full shiatsu treatment.

What To Do: Turn your child onto his back, with his head hanging down slightly, as shown. Hold him by securing his head between your knees and placing his ankles under your arms. Then use both hands to stroke up his yin meridians from his ankles to his fingertips. Your hands will move up the inside of his legs, up the front of his abdomen and chest, and up the inside of his arms from his armpits to the tips of his fingers. Do three times.

Why? A pleasant way to stimulate all yin meridians, and because of the stretching involved, it contributes to healthy lung development. Also good preparation for crawling, as it conveys the idea of how to stretch in crawling.

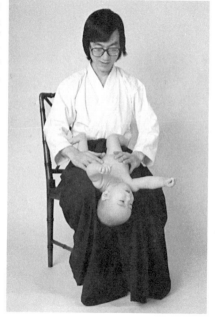

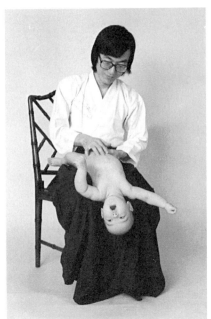

What To Do: Grasp your child securely with one hand under his hips and around one thigh and let his head hang down over your knees. With the palm of your other hand, stroke around his hara clockwise several times, then slide your palm up the middle of his chest to his neck. Repeat the procedure, using your fingers.

Why? Another pleasant way to work on yin meridians, especially effective because the hara is already stretched when you stroke it.

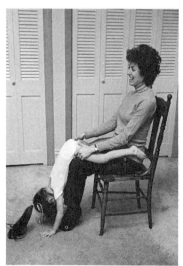

What To Do: With your child on her stomach, grasp one of her thighs securely in one hand and let her hang down from her hips over your knees. Bounce her a minute or two by jiggling your knees up and down. Then, . . .

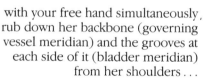

with your free hand simultaneously, rub down her backbone (governing vessel meridian) and the grooves at each side of it (bladder meridian) from her shoulders . . .

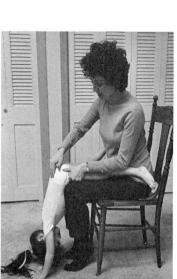

to her hips. Do three times. Repeat, using four fingers, then three fingers, then two fingers. (When using your whole hand or three fingers, your middle finger is over her spine. Otherwise, you stroke just the grooves.)

Why? A fun way to work on the bladder and governing vessel meridians, which, because of the stretching involved, provides deeper stimulation to them and the autonomic nervous system.

Caution: Don't use this procedure until at least half an hour after your child has eaten and don't continue it for more than five minutes, as too much blood goes to the brain. Stop if your child shows discomfort.

In urging you to maintain a positive attitude toward the problems that are so common among children during their first two and a half years, I am not suggesting that you just ignore minor ailments. Quite the contrary. Sickness and structural unevenness, however slight, are always signals that something needs to be done. But when the difficulties are treated early and appropriately, they usually clear up quickly, often through natural measures. Nor do frequent bouts of illness and other physical problems necessarily mean that your child is unhealthy. I was a sickly child myself, but you'd never guess it now.

From the Oriental point of view, the body has natural powers to heal itself. Diarrhea and vomiting, for example, are often its way of cleansing itself of toxins, or calling attention to the need for a change in diet. Fever, if it does not go too high, can be curative. Minor skeletal and joint problems sometimes correct themselves just through a baby's natural squirming and kicking, as if the child knows instinctively how to move to overcome the distortion.

In this chapter I offer you some shiatsu-oriented treatments and other natural Oriental remedies for the most common problems of babies and young children. These remedies should be used when needed in addition to your regular massage program, not as a substitute for it. Most suggested treatments can be used any time after an infant's navel is healed. However, those preceded by an asterisk (*) should not be tried until a baby is four months old or uses his arms to hold his head and shoulders up steadily when in the prone position.

Not all the problems covered here are purely physical. A few involve children's behavior that, though normal during these years, makes life difficult for the family and, if handled inappropriately, could lead eventually to emotional difficulties.

The problems are discussed in alphabetical order. The suggestions I make are meant to be used in conjunction with regular pediatric care. Always check with your child's doctor about any illness or physical symptom that seems serious to you or that your physician has instructed you to call about.

Appetite (Poor)

Use the following procedure to improve appetite and also digestion.

With your child on his stomach, grasp one of his ankles, lift his leg up as shown, and with the fingers of your other hand rub down the front of his leg (stomach meridian) from his groin to his ankle. Do three times, then repeat on the other leg.

Bed-wetting

Healthy children often continue to wet their beds for some time after they can stay dry (mostly) during the day. Some may not outgrow bed-wetting until age five or so. A relaxed, accepting attitude is crucial to helping your child outgrow this at his or her own pace and avoid turning it into a problem.

Since children are more likely to wet their beds when under tension, never scold or punish them in any way when they do. Also, try not to appear anxious or make too big a deal of the issue. Just assure your child that bed-wetting will be outgrown in time.

Some bed-wetting is caused by weakness in the lower hara area. To treat this, try the following two procedures when getting your child ready for bed:

Warm your hands. With one hand under your child's lower back (lumbar region), use your other hand to massage her hara clockwise for several minutes.

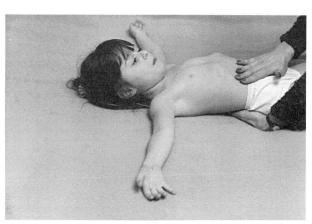

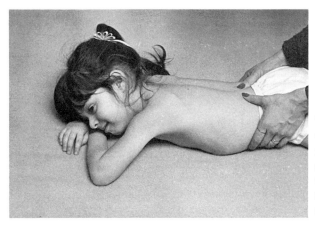

Turn your child on her stomach and with your thumbs massage the tsubos in the groove on each side of her spine next to the last lumbar vertebra (bladder #26). Massage both tsubos at once, using a jiggling motion, for several minutes.

According to Eastern thinking, another possible cause of bed-wetting may be poor functioning of the autonomic nervous system, which, in turn, may be due to a slight spinal distortion. To stimulate healthy development of the autonomic nervous system, give *tingly massage down the back bladder meridian (pages 45 and 48), and use the *exercise on page 82. For procedures that foster correct spinal alignment, see pages *42, 56, 61, *81, and *100.   Encourage as much outdoor play as possible.

Try to avoid giving your child foods containing refined sugar or stimulants such as chocolate, as these are thought to contribute to bed-wetting.

Circulation

The following two procedures help to prevent, as well as to correct poor circulation. Use them in cold weather, or if your child frequently gets cold hands or feet or has a known circulatory problem.

Also see pages *40, *68, and *70 for routines that foster good circulation.

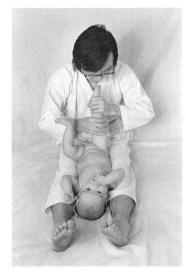

*With your child on his back, feet toward you, grasp one of his ankles and stretch his leg out straight. With your other hand encircle the leg at the top of his thigh and slowly slide your closed hand down to his ankle, squeezing his leg gently as you go. Do three times, then . . .

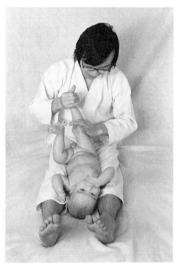

repeat, using your thumb and forefinger— your thumb goes on the back of the leg (bladder meridian) and your forefinger around the front. Repeat the entire procedure on the other leg.

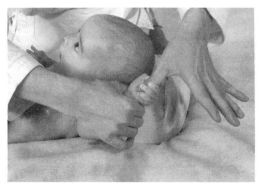

*With your child on his back, head toward you, let him grasp your thumb and stretch his arm out straight. Use your other hand to encircle his arm at the wrist and slowly slide your hand down to his armpit, squeezing gently. Do three times, then . . .

repeat, using your thumb and forefinger—your thumb goes on the inside of the arm (heart constrictor meridian) and your forefinger around the outside. Repeat the entire procedure on the other arm.

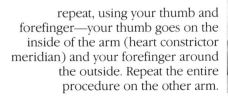

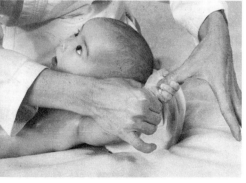

Colds and Other Respiratory Ills

The next two procedures, according to the Oriental viewpoint, help to relieve the discomforts of a cold and to prevent respiratory ailments, including asthma and tuberculosis.

Other procedures that both relieve cold symptoms and help prevent respiratory ills are demonstrated on pages *40–41, *64–65, and *83. *See also*: Nasal Congestion

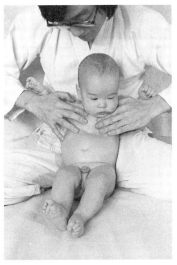

With your child sitting on the floor in front of you, his back against your hara, place four fingers on each side of his breastbone in the spaces between his ribs. Then, slowly . . .

move your fingers out toward his sides, opening his rib cage. Do three times. Use a menthol rub if your child has a cold or his skin is dry. (*This procedure can be done with your child flat on his back, but he may prefer to sit when he has a cold.*)

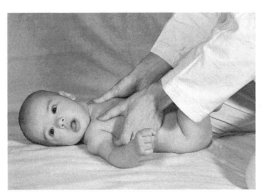

With your child lying on his back, place your thumbs near his arms just below the collarbone (lung #1) and massage the tsubo by gently vibrating your thumbs in place for about three minutes.

Constipation

Failure to have a bowel movement every day does not necessarily mean a child is constipated. The only reliable symptoms of constipation are hard stools combined with difficulty in moving the bowels.

According to Oriental thinking, breast-fed babies are unlikely to become constipated. If they do, the mother should eat more fresh fruits and vegetables and whole grain foods. Constipation in a bottle-fed baby may indicate that the formula needs to be changed or that the child is being overfed—and should be discussed with the baby's doctor.

At all ages, in the traditional Eastern view, the best treatment for constipation is daily shiatsu massage. Exercise is also important. After a child starts to crawl and walk, an environment that provides adequate opportunity for these activities is important. Don't keep your child confined in a carrier or playpen more than is absolutely necessary.

In addition, try these traditional shiatsu remedies:

1) With your child lying on his back, grasp one of his legs at the ankle and extend it up toward his head. Then, with the fingers of your other hand, stroke down the back of his leg (bladder meridian) from his buttocks to his ankle five times. Repeat on the other leg.

2) Place the thumb and forefinger of one hand on each side of your child's spine one vertebra above the pelvic bone (bladder #25) and vibrate in place, exerting gentle pressure, for about two minutes. (This tsubo on the bladder meridian is an associated point for the large intestine meridian.)

3) Place the thumb and forefinger of one hand on either side of your child's navel about an inch out from it (stomach #25) and vibrate as before for about two minutes. Then cover the area with one hand—be sure it is warm—and, as your child exhales, massage gently, pressing down toward the crotch, not straight inward. Continue for about two minutes, pressing only when your child breathes out. Finally, spread your child's legs apart and, while grasping one of his ankles in one hand and pulling his leg out straight, use your other hand to massage the groin area for about two minutes. Repeat on the other side.

4) Place one hand over your child's navel and, without moving it off the navel, gently massage the area clockwise ten times. Rest five minutes, then repeat.

5) Stimulate the rectum by massaging it with your little finger dipped in oil, or with a paper napkin folded to form a cone and dipped in oil.

Convulsions and Epilepsy

Call your doctor if your child has a seizure of any kind. Give first aid as follows:

1) Lay your child on his side in a quiet, cool, spacious area and loosen any tight clothing.

2) Put something that can't be swallowed, such as a folded handkerchief or napkin, between his teeth to prevent him from harming them or biting his tongue. Don't try to force his jaws apart. Wait for this to happen naturally. To encourage the jaws to open, squeeze the nape of his neck (bladder #10) firmly and squeeze his Achilles tendon (at the back of his ankle) very hard. Watch your fingers when inserting anything between his teeth.

3) Cool your hands by holding them in cold water several seconds. Place one hand at the back of your child's neck and squeeze it gently, while holding your other hand on his forehead and pulling his head back slightly. Continue for about three minutes, or until your child regains consciousness.

4) Another way to help your child regain consciousness, in Oriental thinking, is to press hard with two fingertips on his upper lip just beneath his nose (governing vessel #26) for a minute or two.

To prevent seizures and epilepsy, according to the traditional Eastern view, try all the following measures:

1) Avoid high fever (over 104°).

2) Avoid constipation.

3) During your child's daily shiatsu massage, check for any marked difference in temperature between the upper and lower parts of the body or between one side and the other. According to Oriental thinking, any significant unevenness either way in the distribution of body heat indicates a tendency to epilepsy. The *tickling exercise on page 101 helps to encourage symmetrical bilateral distribution of heat. Also, give more massage to the part of the body that is regularly colder.

4) In the Eastern view, if there is a tendency to convulsions or epilepsy, the consumption of highly yang foods (meat and eggs) and highly yin ones (sugar and dairy products) should be kept low. The diet should consist primarily of foods between the two extremes—fish, vegetables and fruits, and especially grains and beans. Also, avoid extremely hot or cold dishes (temperaturewise) and very spicy and sour foods. However, if the lower part of a child's body is colder than the upper part, putting fresh grated ginger in the food is recommended.

Crankiness

To calm a tired, crying, or cranky child, try the next two procedures. They are traditional shiatsu routines used with adults to relieve a headache.

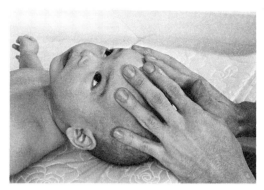

With your child in the same position, place both hands next to each other on top of his head, with your fingers on his forehead. Slowly slide your fingers sideways across his temples and down to the tips of his ears. Do three times. Then, . . .

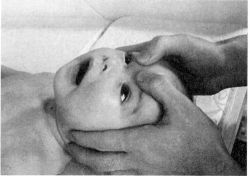

use your thumbs to stroke the same way three times. Finally, . . .

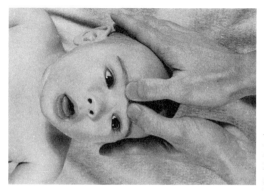

with your palms and fingers encasing his head, as shown, massage his forehead with your thumbs for several minutes.

Warm your hands. With your child on his back, place one hand on his forehead and vibrate it soothingly, while rubbing clockwise around his hara with your other hand for several minutes.

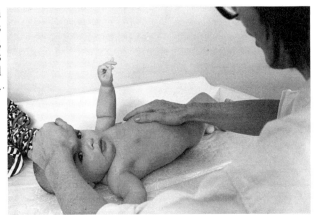

Crying at Night

Normal, healthy babies and young children often wake up crying at night after they have given up night feedings. Parents must always go to a child and soothe him when this happens. The comfort and reassurance their presence provides is essential to children's healthy emotional development. Also, going to the child is the only way to be sure that nothing is really wrong with him.

However, instead of picking up your child to comfort him, try using the techniques for head and hara massage demonstrated in the preceding section (Crankiness). Or use both hands, well warmed, to massage the entire hara area clockwise (page 36) for several minutes.

If children are comforted without being picked up, they tend to go back to sleep again more quickly and cry less frequently at night. Routine massage every day also helps them to sleep undisturbed through the night.

With a child who is especially prone to crying at night, try giving a *"fold and roll" treatment (page 40) down the back bladder meridian just before bedtime.

See also: Sleep (Inducing)

Diaper Rash

The *procedure shown on page 72 helps both to relieve and prevent this problem. Use it in combination with the following treatment.

With your child on his back, on the floor or changing table, hold one of his knees out to the side, uncreasing the groin area, and with the fingers of your other hand, gently massage the area with warm oil for several minutes. Repeat on the other side.

Diarrhea

Diarrhea is often nature's way of cleansing the system of poisons or excessive amounts of food. Breast-fed babies are less subject to this problem than bottle-fed ones. If it occurs in a breast-fed baby, the mother may be eating too much hotly spiced food, or need to make some other change in her diet. However, it may be due to an infection. In any case, it can quickly cause serious dehydration and be extremely dangerous, especially in babies.

Always call your doctor if your child has more than two loose stools in a row. You can use the diagnostic procedure on page 53 to check whether dehydration is occurring.

Besides calling your doctor, try these procedures:

1) Stimulate bladder #25 as demonstrated on page 91.

2) With your thumbs, exert moderate jiggling pressure on stomach #34, on the front of your child's legs slightly above the kneecap.

3) Warm your hands and, with your child on his back, place one hand on his hara, just below the navel, and the other hand under

his lower back. Massage clockwise around the hara area below the navel for several minutes. If the hara feels cold, use a hot hard-boiled egg wrapped in a napkin to rub around the navel for several minutes.

Fainting

To help a child regain consciousness after fainting, use procedure #4, first aid for convulsions (page 92).

Heart Functioning

The following procedure helps to regulate heart functioning and calm down a nervous child. Use it along with daily shiatsu massage if your child tends to be high-strung.

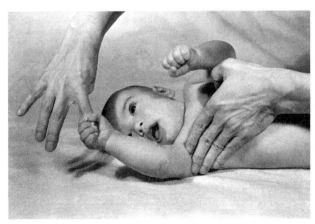

With your child on his back, let him grasp your forefinger or thumb. Pull his arm up toward his head as shown, and with the fingers of your other hand gently massage his armpit (heart meridian #1) with warm oil for several minutes. Repeat on the other side.

Hernia

Consult your doctor if you suspect your child has a hernia.

Parents can sometimes prevent a weak spot in the abdominal area from developing into a true hernia by placing one hand, or finger, on the spot whenever a child cries and pressing firmly enough to prevent bulging. This protects the weak spot and gives it a chance to heal itself gradually.

The routine for groin massage on page 95 helps prevent and alleviate weakness in this area. However, complete shiatsu massage every day, which helps to strengthen the whole body, is more effective than treating one area alone.

Hiccups

Try the procedure for opening the rib cage (page 90) to relieve this condition.

Hip-Joint Problems

The diagnostic procedure for identifying hip-joint problems (page 61) is also a way to help alleviate them. Finish it off by grasping both your child's knees and rotating them up toward his chest, out, and around for several minutes.

Of course, if you think your child has such a problem, bring it to the attention of your doctor.

Hyperactivity

Often children are considered hyperactive when there is nothing medically wrong with them. They are just active at the "wrong time," or so active all the time that they get on adults' nerves.

The traditional Oriental way of dealing with very active children involves:

1) Complete shiatsu massage every day in a tranquil atmosphere—soft light, soft voice, soft music (or total quiet).

2) Daily use of the *tickling routine shown on page 101—but only if the child enjoys this—to promote good development of the autonomic nervous system and healthy discharge of energy.

3) As much outdoor play as possible, to allow the child to enjoy being active and use up energy constructively.

4) A diet that excludes all food additives; is low on overstimulating foods such as chocolate, peanuts, hotly spiced dishes, and those containing refined sugar; limits animal protein; and relies primarily on foods derived from grains and beans and on vegetables for protein.

Nasal Congestion

When your child has a stopped-up nose, try the following procedure before resorting to nose drops.
   This also works for adults.

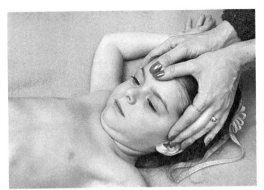

With your child on her back, place
your thumbs next to each other on
the center of her forehead.
Slowly . . .

slide them down along each side of
her nose, then . . .

out across her cheekbones to her
ears. Do three or more times, and
repeat as needed.

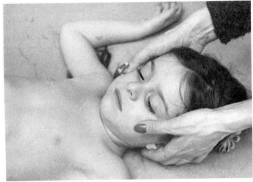

Premature Babies

As indicated at the beginning of this book, daily shiatsu massage is especially important for premature babies, to strengthen all their organs and limbs and help prevent developmental problems. Use a gauze pad or folded small towel to stroke the meridians. Aim for three complete massages a day until your baby can hold his head and shoulders up steadily when in the prone position. After that, other procedures in the book may be incorporated into your regular massage program, according to your child's individual needs and interests.

Rash Under the Arms

The procedure demonstrated on page 69 helps both to relieve and prevent this condition.

Rash Under the Chin

To relieve and prevent rash in this area during a baby's first year or so of life, use the routine shown here several times a day.

With your baby on his back, head toward you, use both hands to rub up his neck from his shoulders to his chin, tilting his chin back gently to smooth out all the creases around his neck. Continue for several minutes. Use warm oil if you like.

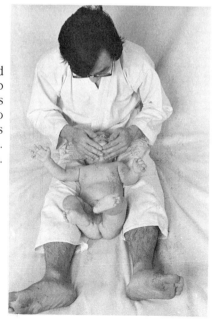

Sleep (Inducing)

There are times when our children don't want to go to sleep at
night or nap during the day, but we are ready for them to do it.
Here is a traditional Oriental procedure that is supposed to make
your baby fall asleep at such times. (Unfortunately, it won't work if
your baby isn't really sleepy.)
See also: Crying at Night

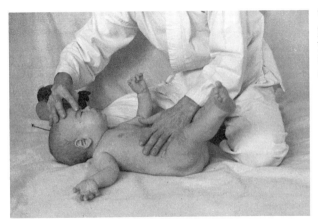

With your child on his back, gently
press the bridge of his nose between
your thumb and forefinger, while
using your other hand to rub his hara
clockwise for several minutes.

Spinal Distortion

Minor distortions of the spine are more common in babies and
young children than is generally recognized. They usually
disappear in time, especially with the help of shiatsu massage and
exercises. Of course, if you suspect a problem, discuss it with your
child's physician. Also try these measures:

1) With a bottle-fed baby, be sure not to hold the bottle in the
same hand for every feeding. Alternate hands, so that your baby's
position is changed regularly, as with breast-feeding.

2) Switch the position of your child's bed at intervals to
encourage him to spend equal time lying on each side. Children

tend to favor one side over the other, depending on which side faces the wall.

3) Use a hard mattress in your child's crib, carriage, and bed.

4) Encourage your child to walk barefoot on uneven ground, such as a pebbly beach, to foster good spinal alignment.

5) To treat (and prevent) minor distortions, also try the procedures demonstrated on the following pages: *42–43, 54, 56, 61, *81, and *85.

6) The *tickling routine shown next is especially good for alleviating minor problems. It encourages children to use their own intuitive knowledge of how to move to overcome slight distortions.

*Sit on your legs Japanese style, with your child on her back in front of you and her head held firmly between your knees. Use both hands to tickle both her sides along the edge of her ribs. As she laughs and wriggles around, she will instinctively move her limbs and torso in ways that tend to correct any distortion.

Caution: Don't do this if your child doesn't enjoy it.

Teething Discomfort

Biting on something hard helps to relieve the pain of cutting a tooth and speed up the process. Babies should be given something they can safely chew on when they start teething. In Japan the traditional teething ring was a ring of dried squid threaded on string and hung around the child's neck. Since I like the idea of a teething object that tastes good, when my son started to teethe, I gave him rings of toasted dried squid to chew on, and he took to this.

Here are two shiatsu remedies for teething discomfort:

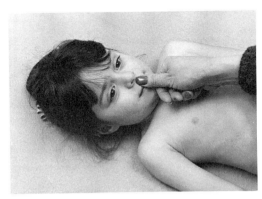

With your child on her back, place one thumb on the center of her upper lip just below her nose (governing vessel #26) and exert gentle pressure, jiggling your thumb for a minute or two. Then, . . .

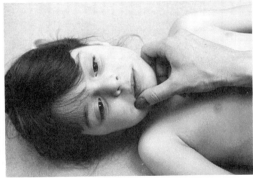

gradually move your thumb, still jiggling, all the way around your child's mouth along the line of her gums. Do two or three times.

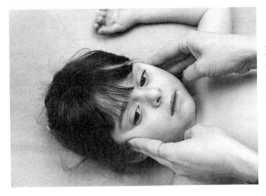

Place three fingers on each of your child's jaws next to her ears and massage the jaws by jiggling your fingers for several minutes.

You can also massage the gums directly with your finger, but you may get bitten this way.

Underactive Child

Children may be chronically listless because of poor appetite or failure to assimilate food properly. For how to improve appetite and digestion, see page 86.

Another cause of chronic lethargy may be failure to breathe deeply enough. The suggested remedies for colds and other respiratory ills (page 90) will encourage deep breathing and healthy lung development.

Sleeping on a mattress that is too soft can also lead to a lowered activity level, because it deters children from moving around in their sleep as much as they normally would. This leaves them more tired than they should be upon awakening. A soft mattress can also cause minor distortions of the spine and autonomic nervous system—another source of lowered energy.

A traditional shiatsu remedy for listlessness is auricular therapy (page 34). Use it twice a day. Also make your daily massage more stimulating by using some of the *techniques in chapter 6 or *applying a little more pressure as you stroke the meridians.

Since chronic lethargy may be a symptom of a dietary deficiency or an undetected organic problem, talk to your doctor about it if it persists over a period of time.

Vomiting

Like diarrhea, vomiting is often a natural mechanism for eliminating poison from the system, or can be due to overfeeding. Always consult your doctor if the vomiting is "projectile," or if your child has a fever.

Also try this traditional shiatsu remedy: With your child sitting or lying on his right side, place one palm on his upper hara slightly below the breastbone, and with your other hand gently massage the area on his back around his left shoulder blade, moving down from the groove next to his spine and out to his side (back stomach area—see "map of the back," page 39). Continue for several minutes. Be sure that your hands are warm.

If your child vomits because he is emotionally upset, place one hand around the back of his neck and hold his neck gently for several minutes. Be sure your hands are warm for both techniques.

Walking Difficulties

Some normal, healthy children walk early, some late. They do it when they are developmentally ready to, and by the time they are three, a person unfamiliar with their histories cannot tell whether a child walked early, late, or in between. So don't push this. If your baby isn't walking by eighteen months, talk over the situation with your doctor.

However, do be sure to use the diagnostic procedure for detecting hip-joint problems (page 61) regularly, at least twice a week. Also check regularly for spinal distortion (pages 54–56).

After your baby is a year old, if he is not walking, include the *tickling routine (page 101) in your daily massage and exercise program—provided he enjoys it—even if he has no discernible spinal or other structural problem. This routine helps a child work in his own way to achieve the coordination and structural strength needed to walk.

When children start walking, they may walk on their toes at times. This need not indicate a problem. But if it persists, and especially if your child *always* walks this way, discuss it with your doctor. It may mean that the Achilles tendons are too tight. To stretch the Achilles tendons, use the foot routine for this (pages 29–31) and *swing your child by the ankles (page 81). Also, while he lies on his back, grasp both his knees, one in each hand, and rotate them up against his chest, out, and around for several minutes.

According to Oriental diagnosis, tight Achilles tendons (and some other muscle problems) may be due to liver damage sustained before birth because of drugs taken by the mother or poor diet during pregnancy. Therefore, give extra shiatsu massage along the liver meridian (page 13) and the bladder meridian (page 10).